Fourth Print Edition [4.0] -1438 h. (2017 c.e.)

Copyright © 1438 H./2017 C.E.
Taalib al-Ilm Educational Resources

http://taalib.com
Learn Islaam, Live Islaam.SM

Requests to the Publisher for permission should be addressed to the Permissions Department, Taalib al-Ilm Educational Resources by e-mail: **service@taalib.com**.

Taalib al-Ilm Education Resources products are made available through distributors worldwide. To view a list of current distributors in your region, or information about our distributor/referral program please visit our website. Discounts on bulk quantities of our products are available to community groups, religious institutions, and other not-for-profit entities, inshAllaah. For details and discount information, contact the special sales department by e-mail: **service@taalib.com**.

The publisher requests that any corrections regarding translations or knowledge based issues, be sent to us at: **service@taalib.com**. Readers should note that internet web sites offered as citations and/or sources for further information may have changed or no longer be available between the time this was written and when it is read.

We publish a variety of full text and free preview edition electronic ebook formats. Some content that appears in print may not be available in electronic book versions.

ISBN EAN-13:   978-1-938117-55-8   [Soft cover Print Edition]

From the Publisher

Golden Words Upon Golden Words...For Every Muslim.

"Imaam al-Barbahaaree, may Allaah have mercy upon him said:

May Allaah have mercy upon you! Examine carefully the speech of everyone you hear from in your time particularly. So do not act in haste and do not enter into anything from it until you ask and see: Did any of the Companions of the Prophet, may Allaah's praise and salutations be upon him, speak about it, or did any of the scholars? So if you find a narration from them about it, cling to it, do not go beyond it for anything and do not give precedence to anything over it and thus fall into the Fire.

Explanation by Sheikh Saaleh al-Fauzaan, may Allaah preserve him:

'Do not be hasty in accepting as correct what you may hear from the people especially in these later times. As now there are many who speak about so many various matters, issuing rulings and ascribing to themselves both knowledge and the right to speak. This is especially the case after the emergence and spread of new modern day media technologies. Such that everyone now can speak and bring forth that which is in truth worthless; by this meaning words of no true value - speaking about whatever they wish in the name of knowledge and in the name of the religion of Islaam. It has even reached the point that you find the people of misguidance and the members of the various groups of misguidance and deviance from the religion speaking as well. Such individuals have now become those who speak in the name of the religion of Islaam through means such as the various satellite television channels. Therefore be very cautious!

It is upon you oh Muslim, and upon you oh student of knowledge individually, to verify matters and not rush to embrace everything and anything you may hear. It is upon you to verify the truth of what you hear, asking, 'Who else also makes this same statement or claim?', 'Where did this thought or concept originate or come from?', 'Who is its reference or source authority?'. Asking what are the evidences which support it from within the Book and the Sunnah? And inquiring where has the individual who is putting this forth studied and taken his knowledge from? From who has he studied the knowledge of Islaam?

Each of these matters requires verification through inquiry and investigation, especially in the present age and time. As it is not every speaker who should rightly be considered a source of knowledge, even if he is well spoken and eloquent, and can manipulate words captivating his listeners. Do not be taken in and accept him until you are aware of the degree and scope of what he possesses of knowledge and understanding. As perhaps someone's words may be few, but possess true understanding, and perhaps another will have a great deal of speech yet he is actually ignorant to such a degree that he doesn't actually posses anything of true understanding. Rather he only has the ability to enchant with his speech so that the people are deceived. Yet he puts forth the perception that he is a scholar, that he is someone of true understanding and comprehension, that he is a capable thinker, and so forth. Through such means and ways he is able to deceive and beguile the people, taking them away from the way of truth.

Therefore what is to be given true consideration is not the amount of the speech put forth or that one can extensively discuss a subject. Rather the criterion that is to be given consideration is what that speech contains within it of sound authentic knowledge, what it contains of the established and transmitted principles of Islaam. As perhaps a short or brief statement which is connected to or has a foundation in the established principles can be of greater benefit than a great deal of speech which simply rambles on, and through hearing you don't actually receive very much benefit from.

This is the reality which is present in our time; one sees a tremendous amount of speech which only possesses within it a small amount of actual knowledge. We see the presence of many speakers yet few people of true understanding and comprehension.' "

[The eminent major scholar Sheikh Saaleh al-Fauzaan, may Allaah preserve him- 'A Valued Gift for the Reader Of Comments Upon the Book Sharh as-Sunnah', page 102-103]

❨ *Is not He better than your so-called gods, He Who originates creation and shall then repeat it, and Who provides for you from heaven and earth? Is there any god with Allaah? Say: 'Bring forth your proofs, if you are truthful.'* ❩-(Surah an-Naml: 64)

Explanation: ❨ ***Say: "Bring forth your proofs..***❩ This is a command for the Prophet, may Allaah praise and salutation be upon him, to rebuke them immediately after they had put forward their own rebuke. Meaning: '*Say to them: bring your proof, whether it is an intellectual proof or a proof from transmitted knowledge, that would stand as evidence that there is another with Allaah, the Most Glorified and the Most Exalted*'. Additionally, it has been said that it means: '*Bring your proof that there is anyone other than Allaah, the Most High, who is capable of doing that which has been mentioned from His actions, the Most Glorified and the Most Exalted.*' ❨ *if you are truthful,* ❩ meaning, in this claim. From this it is derived that a claim is not accepted unless clearly indicated by evidences."

[*Tafseer al-'Aloosee: vol. 15, page 14*]

Sheikh Rabee'a Ibn Hadee Umair al-Madkhalee, may Allaah preserve him said,

'It is possible for someone to simply say, "*So and so said such and such.*" However we should say, "*Produce your proof.*" So why did you not ask them for their proof by saying to them: "*Where was this said?*" Ask them questions such as this, as from your weapons are such questions as: "*Where is this from? From which book? From which cassette?...*" '

[*The Overwhelming Falsehoods of 'Abdul-Lateef Bashmeel' page 14*]

The guiding scholar Imaam Sheikh 'Abdul-'Azeez Ibn Abdullah Ibn Baaz, may Allaah have mercy upon him, said,

'It is not proper that any intelligent individual be mislead or deceived by the great numbers from among people from the various countries who engage in such a practice. As the truth is not determined by the numerous people who engage in a matter, rather the truth is known by the Sharee'ah evidences. Just as Allaah the Most High says in Surah al-Baqarah, ❨ ***And they say, "None shall enter Paradise unless he be a Jew or a Christian." These are only their own desires. Say "Produce your proof if you are truthful."***❩-(Surah al-Baqarah: 111) And Allaah the Most High says ❨ ***And if you obey most of those on the earth, they will mislead you far away from Allaah's path. They follow nothing but conjectures, and they do nothing but lie.***❩-(Surah al-'Ana'an: 116)'

[*Collection of Rulings and Various Statements of Sheikh Ibn Baaz -Vol. 1 page 85*]

Sheikh Muhammad Ibn 'Abdul-Wahaab, may Allaah have mercy upon him, said,

'Additionally verify that knowledge held regarding your beliefs, distinguishing between what is correct and false within it, coming to understand the various areas of knowledge of faith in Allaah alone and the required disbelief in all other objects of worship. You will certainly see various different matters which are called towards and enjoined; so if you see that a matter is in fact one coming from Allaah and His Messenger, then this is what is intended and is desired that you possess. Otherwise, Allaah has certainly given you that which enables you to distinguish between truth and falsehood, if Allaah so wills.

Moreover, this writing of mine- do not conceal it from the author of that work; rather present it to him. He may repent and affirm its truthfulness and then return to the guidance of Allaah, or perhaps if he says that he has a proof for his claims, even if that is only a single statement or if he claims that within my statements there is something unsupported, then request his evidence for that assertion. After this if there is something which continues to cause uncertainty or is a problem for you, then refer it back to me, so that then you are aware of both his statement and mine in that issue. We ask Allaah to guide us, you, and all the Muslims to that which He loves and is pleased with.'

[Personal Letters of Sheikh Muhammad Ibn 'Abdul-Wahaab- Conclusion to Letter 20]

Sheikh 'Abdullah Ibn 'Abdur-Rahman Abu Bateen, may Allaah have mercy upon him, said,

'And for an individual, if it becomes clear to him that something is the truth, he should not turn away from it and or be discouraged simply due to the few people who agree with him and the many who oppose him in that, especially in these latter days of this present age.

If the ignorant one says: *"If this was the truth so and so and so and so would have been aware of it!"* However this is the very claim of the disbelievers, in their statement found in the Qur'aan ❧ **If it had truly been good, they would not have preceded us to it!"** ❧-(Surah al-Ahqaaf: 11) and in their statement ❧ **Is it these whom Allaah has favored from amongst us?"** ❧-(Surah al-Ana'am: 53). Yet certainly as Alee Ibn Abee Taalib, may Allaah be pleased with him, stated *"Know the truth and then you will know it's people."* But for the one who generally stands upon confusion and uncertainty, then every doubt swirls around him. And if the majority of the people were in fact upon the truth today, then Islaam would not be considered strange, yet by Allaah it is today seen as the most strange of affairs!"

[Durar As-Sanneeyyah -vol. 10, page 400]

Whispers of Paradise (1): A Muslim Woman's Life Journal

Developed by:
Taalib al-Ilm Educational Resources Staff

Table of Contents

Verily, all praise is due to Allaah, we praise Him, we seek His assistance and we ask for His forgiveness. We seek refuge in Him from the evils of our souls and the evils of our actions. Whoever Allaah guides, no one can lead him astray and whoever is caused to go astray, there is no one that can guide him. I bear witness that there is no deity worthy of worship except Allaah alone with no partners. And I bear witness that Muhammad is His worshipper and Messenger, peace and salutations be upon him, his household, his Companions, and all those who follow his guidance until the day of Judgment. To proceed:

Allaah, the Most Merciful has informed us that ﴾ *Indeed whosoever purifies himself shall achieve success* ﴿- (Surah al-A'laa:14), While explaining this verse the guiding scholar Sheikh Muhammad Ibn Saaleh al-'Utheimeen, may Allah have mercy upon him, stated, "the word which means "achieves success" is derived from the word 'al-falaah' which is a inclusive term, which indicates: the achievement of what is desired and sought after, as well as being saved from what is detested and feared. This is the meaning of 'al-falaah'. And it is a comprehensive term indicating that which encompasses every form of good and that which repels every form of evil." (Tafseer of The Guiding Scholar Muhammad Ibn Saaleh al-'Utheimen, page 11). We live in an age that is filled with numerous so-called self-help and self-improvement systems; yet most modern women still find that they have not found the contentment and success promised by these various specialized paths of 'personal self fulfillment'. Neither have they found it through the indiscriminate adoption of Western values which encourage their focus to become the pursuit of personal gratification, often as a consumer through the acquisition of material possessions. Many women the world over have realized that so much of what is offered is mostly shine and little substance, and its price is far higher than what one receives in return. Accordingly it is upon every Muslim woman today to realize that true success and contentment will only come through fulfilling the purpose for which she and every other human being was created- the worship of Allaah alone without partner or associate.

Yet then the question is, what is 'worship'? Sheikh al-Islaam Ibn Taymeeyah, may Allaah have mercy upon him, was asked about the statement of Allaah, the Most Glorified and the Most Exalted, ﴾ *Oh mankind! Worship your Lord* ..﴿- (Surah al-Baqarah:21) with the questioner saying, "What is worship and what are its branches? Is the entire religion considered worship or not? What is the reality of subservience to Allaah? Is it the highest position one can attain in this life and the next world, or are there positions higher than this? Please explain this thoroughly to us." He replied,

"All praise is due to Allaah Lord of all the worlds, worship is the comprehensive name for everything that Allaah loves and is pleased with, from statements and actions, both internal and external. This includes ritual prayer, obligatory charity, obligatory fasting, pilgrimage to the house of Allaah, speaking truthfully, fulfilling the trust, acting kindly towards one's parents and maintaining family relations, the honoring of agreements, enjoining what is good and forbidding wrongdoing, striving against the disbelievers and the hypocrites, good behavior towards ones neighbor, the poor, orphans, and towards travelers, proper guardianship over both people and animals, supplicating to Allaah and engaging in His remembrance, recitation of the Qur'an , and other similar examples from acts of worship.

Likewise it encompasses the love of Allaah and His Messenger, the fearing of Allaah and reliance upon Him, the making the entire religion solely for His sake alone, and patience with what Allaah has decreed, and thankfulness for His blessings, and being pleased with His rulings and guidance..." (Majmou' al-Fataawa 10/150)

Therefore we see that the worship of our Lord can only be performed through striving and struggling to adhere to the guidance of Islaam in every matter, both small and large. And without question the happiness of the believing woman lies in recognizing and committing herself to understanding this path of comprehensive worship in every area of her life, and then steadily walking upon it with knowledge of: where she stands, where she is headed and how she can get there. The only true map and guide that can be used in this is that revealed guidance which Allaah sent down to direct and guide each and every one of us; that guidance which He has perfected and preserved in the guidance of the Noble Qur'an and the pure Sunnah, and the examples of steadfast believers showing how to live that guidance in every age that He has blessed us with. One who investigates finds that the practice of self-examination and self-scrutiny was a foundation of the efforts of self-purification and seeking closeness to the Lord of the worlds, as found in the lives of the final Prophet, his noble Companions, those first guided generations, as well as every striving guided Muslim who followed their straight path until today. The result was that, with Allaah's support, they made Islaam a reality in their own lives and a reality in the world around them.

This life journal is intended to be an aid and support for any Muslim woman who in her efforts seeks to come closer to Allaah and what He loves. The concept was first suggested and implemented as a supplementary tool by our sister Umm Mujaahid Khadijah Bint Lacina in a class she taught and then within the book which was developed from the class "Al-Waajibaat: The Obligatory Matters" as a means of encouraging the class participants to question and assess the individual realities of their faith in both its essential principles and fundamental practices. The objective was that each student might better understand personally and privately where they stood in light of the guidance that our Most Merciful Lord sent down to us through His final messenger Muhammad, may Allaah praise and salutation be upon him, his household, and his Companions, and all those who followed his guidance. As how many Muslims today have a faulty "personal" understanding and practice of Islaam that perhaps would not be even recognized by our beloved Prophet if it was shown to him?! How often do we actually weigh what and who we love or hate against the standard of revealed guidance we claim as Muslims? How easy and comfortable the trap of Shaytaan has become today, where one simply remains upon his or her desires while justifying them through comfortable excuses and pleasing words and labels without inspecting and questioning one's self. The eminent senior scholar Imaam Abdul-Azeez Ibn Abdullah Ibn Baaz, may Allaah have mercy upon him, said,

"From the significant trials and tribulations is when someone works, believing that he is upon guidance, believing that he is benefiting in bringing good, when in reality he is harming the people. Just as Allaah says, ﴾ *Say: "Shall We tell you the greatest losers in respect of their deeds? Those whose efforts have been wasted in this life while they thought that they were acquiring good by their deeds!* ﴿– (Surah Kahf: 103-104) And this is a tremendous loss; that one strives diligently with his wealth, time, and various types of efforts, but all of which in reality does not benefit him, but only harms him. It is from the matters that anger Allaah and which prevent the spread of the truth. So certainly it is one of the tremendous losses and we ask Allaah for safety and well-being.

Therefore the person of intelligence brings himself to account and struggles within himself. He considers carefully and is not silent within himself nor heedless of this. He considers what it is that he is endeavoring upon and what he is sending forth for the next world- thinking and considering carefully. Just as the Most Exalted says, *Oh you who believe! Fear Allaah and keep your duty to Him. And let every person look to what he has sent forth for tomorrow, and fear Allaah. Verily, Allaah is All-Aware of what you do. And be not like those who forgot Allaah (i.e. became disobedient to Allaah) and He caused them to forget their own selves, (let them to forget to do righteous deeds). Those are the rebellious, disobedient to Allaah. Not equal are the dwellers of the Hellfire and the dwellers of the Paradise. It is the dwellers of Paradise that will be successful.* -(Surah al-Hashr: 18-20)

So the person of intelligence proceeds and looks and considers: what has he sent forward, what has he done for the next world, and his next life? What has he put forward which opposes misguidance, what has he undertaken for the success and contentment of his wife, children, neighbor, and society? Do not be heedless! It is required that he continually and constantly questions and considers matters. Is he in a state of loss or one of profit and success? Is he content or in misery? Is he upon guidance or misguidance?

Consider and evaluate yourself all the time, and make yourself adhere to the truth which you understand- hold fast to the truth by preserving your congregational prayer, by paying the obligatory zakaat charity, by good treatment to your parents, by maintaining family ties, by staying away from the different forms of immoral behavior, and by leaving evil companionship. Similarly, calling yourself to account for shortcomings- so the one who drinks intoxicants calls himself to account and abandons those intoxicants completely, the one who sits with people who are bad companions should call himself to account and distance himself from them. Look carefully at your actions; are they benefiting or harming you? Are you working in that which will benefit you in the next life or acting in a way that will lead to Hellfire? Indeed, call yourself to account." (taken from "A Lecture Discussing the Ideological War")

And the guiding scholar and imaam of our time Sheikh Muhammad Ibn Saaleh al-'Utheimeen, may Allaah have mercy upon him, said,

"Also from your contemplating Allaah is that you do so with regards to your secrets and what is in your heart. Look to what is in your heart! Associating partners with Allaah, showing off, deviations, jealousy, hatred and dislike displayed towards the Muslims, love of the disbelievers and other such things that Allaah is not pleased with. Scrutinize and be attentive to your heart for Allaah has said, *Indeed We created man, and We know what his own self whispers to him.* -(Surah Qaaf:16) So contemplate Allaah in these three places, in your actions, your saying and your heart so that your contemplation may be complete. This is why, when the Prophet, may Allaah's praise and salutations be upon him, was asked about Ihsaan, he replied, *{...that you worship Allaah as if you see Him, and if you do not see Him, then indeed He sees you}*. Worship Allaah as if you see Him and witness Him with the eye, and if you do not see Him then go to the next station below this is remembering that indeed He sees you. So the first station is to worship Him out of hope and desire. The next is to worship Him out of fear and awe this is why he said, *{and if you do not see Him, then indeed He sees you.}* .As such it is necessary for the person to contemplate His Lord and that he know that Allaah is Watching over you. Anything that you say or do or keep secret, Allaah, Exalted is He, Knows it." (from his explanation of 'Riyaadh as-Saaliheen')

Similarly Sheikh Rabee'a Ibn Haadee, may Allaah preserve him, reminds us in "The Poor Present Condition of the Muslims & the Path to its Rectification"

"However today, do we restrict ourselves to what is found in the Book of Allaah? Oh my brother, it is essential that each one of us calls himself to account and judges himself saying, 'Do I stand upon the position of truth or as one who is mistaken regarding the issue of such and such individual and the matter of the condition of so and so? In this do I stand upon the truth or upon a mistake?'

You will not arrive at the truth except if you surrender to Allaah and place yourself in compliance with Allaah, the Most Glorified and the Most Exalted, and truly judge yourself according to the Book of Allaah and the Sunnah of Messenger of Allaah, may Allaah's praise and salutations be upon him. It is only then that it is possible to become someone who truly stands in conformance with that guidance, when it becomes possible for you to return back to the truth in everything. But if you give free rein to yourself, giving way and indulging in whatever you desire, then you cannot stand in conformance with guidance in any way, not towards the Book of Allaah nor towards the Sunnah of the Messenger of Allaah, may Allaah's praise and salutations be upon him. And so misguidance will certainly come to dominate you."

Allaah, the Most High, has clearly informed us about this dangerous reality, those who exchange His guidance with the easy way of simply following their desires where He says, *...And who is more astray than one who follows his own lusts, without guidance from Allaah? Verily, Allaah guides not the people who are wrong doers, disobedient to Allaah.*– (Surah al-Qasas:050). And Allaah, the Most High calls us to consider and compare in His statement, *Is the one who is on a clear proof from his Lord, like those for whom the evil deeds that they do are beautified for them, while they only follow their own evil desires?*– (Surah Muhammad:014). Likewise Allaah, the Most High also warns us, *Have you seen him who takes his own vain desires as his god? And Allaah knowing him as such, left him astray, and sealed his hearing and his heart, and put a cover on his sight. Who then will guide him after Allaah? Will you not then remember?*– (Surah al-Jaathiyah:023)

Imaam Ibn Qayyim, may Allaah have mercy upon him, has encompassed many insightful transmitted statements from the first esteemed generations concerning this essential obligation of and self-examination and accounting which will, with Allaah's permission, benefit every sincere Muslimah who reads, review and ponders them. He said:

"..What is intended here is the mentioning of the cure for the ailment of the heart by the individual taking control over it and what it constantly urges and incites towards, and this has two specific cures:

Firstly, the calling of the heart to account through self-examination and, secondly, the opposing of its desires. As the destruction of one's heart is caused by heedlessness and inattention towards self-examination as well as one's simply conforming to and following its desires. In a hadeeth narrated by Imaam Ahmad and others on the authority of Shadaad Ibn Aws, who said: The Messenger of Allaah, may Allaah's praise and salutations be upon him, said, "The intelligent person is the one who takes command over his soul and strives for what will come after death. And the incompetent person is the one who simply follows his desires and merely hopes for Allaah's mercy." Taking command here means calling his soul to account through self-scrutiny and accounting.

Imaam Ahmad narrates that 'Umar Ibn al-Khattab, may Allah be pleased with him, said, "Call yourselves to account before you are to be taken account of; weigh and assess yourself before you are to be weighed and assessed. As those of you who will be in an easier, comfortable position tomorrow are those who have called themselves to account today, weighing and assessing themselves in preparation for the greatest judgment of that Day in which during your accounting you will not be able to hide anything."

It has also been mentioned that al-Hasan al-Basree said, "You will not achieve the state of truly being a believer until you call yourself to account. What is it that you intend to do? What is it that you intend to eat and drink, and where does it come from? As the transgressor is the one who blindly fumbles forward step after step without calling himself to account for that which he engages in."

Qatadah said about the meaning of the statement of Allaah, *...one who follows his own lusts and whose affair or deeds have been lost.*– (Surah Al-Kahf: 28) "It means that he has ruined himself, and wronged himself by striving to preserve his material wealth at the cost of losing his religion." Al-Hasan said, "The worshiper of Allaah does not leave being in a state of goodness as long as he has that within himself which admonishes him and he is someone who vigorously questions himself about his affairs."

Maymoon Ibn Mihran said, "The worshipper of Allah will not be someone who truly fears Allaah until he stands as someone who more severely calls himself to account than one would question one's partner in a business enterprise." And it has been said that the soul is like a treacherous business partner, in that if you do not question and require his constant accounting he will surely steal away your wealth. Additionally, Maymoon Ibn Mihran said, "The one who fears Allaah is more strenuous in his examination and accounting of himself than one would be towards the disloyal governor or a miserly business partner." And Imaam Ahmad mentioned that Wahb said, "It was recorded in the wisdom which was previously possessed by the family of Prophet Dawud: 'It is only proper that the intelligent person does not neglect four hours: That hour in which he works to make his Lord victorious, that hour in which he takes account of himself, that hour in which he sits individually with his brothers who may inform him of some of his shortcomings, speaking truthfully to him, and that hour in which he struggles to renounce those matters of conflict that stand between himself and his soul in that which his soul has been deceived by and found so appealing. And this last hour is the aide and supporter for the other three hours by which they become more significant or considerable in their affect upon the heart. This has been narrated in an connected format back to the Prophet, may Allaah's praise and salutations be upon him, by Abi Haatim, Ibn Hibaan, and other than him.'" (Note: the various narrations explicitly attributing this back to the Messenger of Allaah, may Allaah's praise and salutations be upon him, have weaknesses as indicated by Sheikh al-Albaanee, may Allaah have mercy upon him, in his notes to the relevant narrations in 'Saheeh Ibn Hibaan' and 'Da'ef at-Taghreeb wa at-Tarheeb')

Al-Ahnaf Ibn Qais came toward a burning lamp and placed his finger within it and then said to himself, "Feel this Oh Haneef, for what you have come to from what you put forth on such and such day, and from what you have come to from what you put forth on such and such other day." 'Umar Ibn al-Khattab wrote to some of those who worked under his authority when he was the Khaleefah saying, "...Call yourself to account in the time of ease before a severe accounting. As the one who takes account of himself in the time of ease before the time of the difficult accounting, his affair ends as one of contentment and happiness; but the one who is distracted by his worldly affairs, and preoccupied with his desires, then his affair ends as one of loss and remorse." ...

...Maalik Ibn Dinaar said, "May Allaah have mercy upon the worshiper who says to himself, 'Aren't you the one who did so and so, aren't you the one who did so and so- then he tightens his hold over himself and he places restrictions upon himself, and makes himself adhere to the Book of Allaah, the Most Glorified and the Most Exalted, and the Sunnah, and in this there is the needed taking command."

The soul in relation to its possessor has been compared to someone who is your partner in financial matters. Just as the profit one strives for in a business partnership will not be achieved except by firstly, clearly setting the conditions of what work your partner must undertake, then secondly examining everything he engages in, both supervising it and inspecting it, then thirdly by taking him to account for completing these actions, then fourthly by preventing him from any transgressions that he is found to be engaged in. Likewise is the case of the soul. Firstly you must place rules and conditions upon it- that it must protect the seven limbs which if one preserves them that is his most important wealth and form of success. As the one who has failed to preserve this essential wealth, how can he even aspire to achieve more and be successful further?! These seven limbs are the eyes, the ears, the mouth, the sexual organs, the hands, and the legs. Together they are a vessel of either possible ruin or of possible success. Within it lies ruin if it is destroyed by neglect and a failure to preserve them, and in it lies success in their protection and using them well. Their preservation is the foundation of every goodness and their neglect is the foundation of every evil. And Allaah the Most High said: *Tell the believing men to lower their gaze from looking at forbidden things, and protect their private parts from illegal sexual acts* - (Surah An-Nur: 30) And Allaah the Most High said: *And walk not on the earth with conceit and arrogance. Verily, you can neither rend nor penetrate the earth, nor can you attain a stature like the mountains in height.* -(Surah Al-Isra': 37) And Allaah has said, *And follow not that of which you have no knowledge. Verily! The hearing, and the sight, and the heart, of each of those you will be questioned by Allaah.* - (Surah Al-Isra':) And Allaah has said, *And say to My worshipers that they should only speak those words that are the best.* - (Surah Al-Isra: 53) And Allaah has said, *Oh you who believe! Keep your duty to Allaah and fear Him, and speak always the truth.* - (Surah Al-Ahzaab: 70) And Allaah has said, *Oh you who believe! Fear Allaah and keep your duty to Him. And let every person look to what he has sent forth for tomorrow* -(Surah Al-Hashr:18)

So after you put these conditions in place to protect these seven body parts, then you next move to examining, supervising, and monitoring them- not simply neglecting them- as if you neglect them even for a moment they will stray into transgression. This is what is truly required, as continuing to be neglectful and heedless leads to carrying forward into transgressions until eventually your most important possession has been lost to you entirely. Therefore whenever you recognize a decrease or lessening in your affairs move yourself towards self examination, such that undertaking this will clarify the reality of where your true profit and loss is to be found. And when you perceive some loss, then you should have the determination to correct it, just as a someone involved in a partnership would correct the actions of his partner: working towards a return to the previous suitable state, maintaining its state of protection and the practice of scrutinizing it through examination, and calling it to account in order to warn it from heedlessness.

And what will assist you in these efforts of scrutiny and self-examination is your understanding that if you strive diligently in this today you will be able to relax regarding it in the future when the full accounting will pass into the control of another, and if he is neglectful of it today that coming accounting will indeed be hard and difficult on him tomorrow. Additionally what also assists you in this is your understanding that the profit and reward to be taken in this transaction is living in the garden of Firdaws in Paradise, and viewing the face of your Lord, how free from all imperfection He is! While failing in these efforts leads to entering Hellfire, and being denied and shielded from seeing Allaah the Most High. Thus if you become certain and convinced of this, then the self account done today becomes easy for him.

So it is required for the steadfast believer in Allaah and the Last Day not be heedless and to call himself to account- forcing himself in all his movements, positions, daily moments, and very footsteps- toward what is correct. For every person his soul's success is the most valuable jewel or possession in his life. There is no possible success if at the cost of this you purchase a treasure from among the treasures of the world, or prevent it from its happiness in the everlasting eternity! Such that the loss of this "wealth" held by these souls have or their companions selling them in exchange for that which only in fact brings forward their destruction - is an extensive and far-reaching loss which nobody would allow except for the most ignorant and foolish of the people, those with the very least of intelligence. Indeed the reality of this tremendous loss will become evident of the Day of Judgment, ❦ *On the Day when every person will be confronted with all the good he has done, and all the evil he has done, he will wish that there were a great distance between him and his evil* ❧– (Surah Aal-'Imran:30)".

(Imaam Ibn Qayyim in his work 'The Yearned for Relief From the Pursuit by Shaytaan', pages 79-84)

From these many insightful narrations which he has presented, may Allaaah have abundant mercy upon him, it should be clear that what is required for every striving Muslimah today, the one truly striving in and upon Islaam, is that she calls to account both herself- as mentioned by Abu Alee at-Thaqafee when he said, "Abu Hafs used to say: The one who does not each moment weigh his situation and condition against scale of the Book of Allaah and the Sunnah, and does not question his very footsteps, then he is not to be considered worthy. (Siyaar 'Alaam an-Nubala: vol. 12, 512) as well as taking the time to question and examine everything which comes from those around her - as was transmitted from Abu Sulaymaan ad-Daaraanee, who said, "Sometimes there occurs in my heart a saying from the saying of the people of today, yet I do not accept it -except when it is supported by two upright witnesses, the Book of Allaah and the Sunnah."(Siyaar 'Alaam an-Nubala: vol. 10, page 183). This life journal is designed to encourage this beneficial self-examination and facilitate its fruit of continuing rectification which self-examination bears if Allaah grants His worshipper success. We hope that through it we are placing our hands side by side with the many other Muslim hands which are striving to support a 'pillar' of our Ummah -the striving Muslim woman. As certainly this is a pillar which so many efforts are being directed towards weakening, and which so many from the enemies of Islaam are working ceaselessly to topple. May Allaah enable every Muslim man and every Muslim woman to always remember why the Muslim woman is so essential to our success and rectification, as our Sheikh Muhammad al-Imaam, may Allaah preserve him, explains so clearly,

*"**The Muslim woman's position among the Muslims cannot be assessed with sufficient value, as she is more precious than everything found upon the face of the earth from material things. And how could this not be, when she brings into maturity our men and raises generations, and from her hand comes forth the guiding sincere scholars who fear Allaah who are the truthful strivers in Allaah's path, as well as producing the best of men, distinguished young men, and wholesome young women. So if the Muslims sacrifice or suffer in relation to the Muslim woman, our institutions are corrupted at their very foundations, our pillars fall from their places, and in this lies the tremendous danger.**"*(From the introduction of his book 'The Immense Plot Again the Muslim Woman')

Constructive comments and corrections are welcomed at lifejournal@taalib.com. We ask Allaah for success and forgiveness for every believing man and believing woman, and that He grant us each success in this world and the next. May the praise and salutations of Allaah be upon the Messenger of Allaah, his household, his Companions, and all those who followed his guidance until the Day of Judgement. I end in the praise of Allaah.

Abu Sukhailah Khalil Ibn-Abelahyi
Taalib al-Ilm Educational Resources

Muharram

1438

OCT 2016

Yawm al-Sabt Saturday	Yawm al-Ahad Sunday	Yawm al-Ithnayn Monday	Yawm ath-Thulatha Tuesday	Yawm al-Arbi'a Wednesday	Yawm al-Khamees Thursday	Yawm al-Jumu'ah Friday
	1 / 2	2 / 3	3 / 4	4 / 5	5 / 6	6 / 7
7 / 8	8 / 9	9 / 10	10 / 11	11 / 12	12 / 13	13 / 14
14 / 15	15 / 16	16 / 17	17 / 18	18 / 19	19 / 20	20 / 21
21 / 22	22 / 23	23 / 24	24 / 25	25 / 26	26 / 27	27 / 28
28 / 29	29 / 30	30 / 31				

"Oh you of little resolve, where do you stand upon this path? Aadam found it difficult and Nuh lamented because of it, while Allaah's Khaleel Ibraaheem was thrown into a pit of fire due to it. Isma'eel was laid upon his side ready to be sacrificed for its sake, and while upon it Yusuf was sold for a cheap price and then falsely cast into prison for many years. Zakareeyah was sawed in half, and Yahya was slaughtered due to it. Ayyub suffered great distress, while Dawud cried copiously, and 'Isaa cured the wretched poor of their diseases and walked with wild beasts due to it. And how many, how many forms of difficulty and hardship did the Messenger Muhammad face while proceeding upon it - yet you live your life through amusements and distractions!"

(Sheikh al-Islaam Ibn Qayyim in his work *"al-Fawaid"*, page 41)

"Say: "Verily, my salaat, my sacrifice, my living, and my dying are for Allaah, the Lord of the all the worlds. He has no partner. And of this I have been commanded, and I am the first of the Muslims." (Surah al-An'aam:162)

Muharram

1st

Notes

Therefore be diligent in ensuring that you only have one priority- that priority being Allaah alone, as in this objective is a worshipper's happiness. The one who is in this state finds that he is in a present state of contentment, having entered a worldly paradise before reaching the Paradise of the Hereafter. As some people have said, "Certainly, the heart passes through times during which I say, 'If the people of Paradise are in a state like this, then indeed they are enjoying a superior life.'" Another one has said, "Indeed, there times in which my heart seems to dance with happiness." And another one said, "Oh the poor ones of this world! They are those who depart from this world without having tasted the best of what is found within it." So it was said, "And what is the best of what can be found within it?" He replied, "Truly knowing about Allaah, having love for Him, finding contentment in nearness to Him, and being delighted in your meeting with Him."

(A Treatise Written by Ibn Qayyim to One of his Brothers, page 34)

Notes

Abu Hurairah reported that the Prophet, may Allaah's praise and salutations be upon him, said, "The worst of my Ummah are those who talk a lot, those who are speak loudly without cause, and those who strive to seem eloquent in speech. The best of my community are the best of them in character." (Authenticated by Sheikh Al-Albaanee in Saheeh 'Adab al-Mufrad: 982)

Muharram
3rd

Notes

Wahb Ibn al-Ward said, "A man came to Wahb Ibn Munabeh and said, 'I have decided and said to myself that I should not mix with the people.' He replied, "Don't do so, as it is required that you have dealings with the people, and that they have dealings with you. They have things which they need from you and you likewise have the same from them. However, be among them as a seemingly deaf person who listens carefully, a seemingly blind person who sees well, and a seemingly silent one who actually speaks expressively. (Siyaar 'Alaam an-Nubala: vol. 4, page 550)

Notes

Al-Khateeb al-Baghdaadee said, "It is fitting that he takes care in acquiring knowledge and that he should not take too much at one time. Rather, he should take a little at a time, such that he can bear it, memorize it and be able to understand it. Because Allaah says, "And those who disbelieve say: 'Why is the Qur'an not sent down to him all at once?' Thus is it sent down in parts- that We may strengthen your heart thereby. And We have revealed it to you gradually, in stages." (Surah al-Furqaa :32)" (Al-Faqeeh wa al-Mutafaqqih)

Muharram
5th

Notes

Abu Hurairah reported that the Messenger of Allaah, may Allaah's praise and salutations be upon him, said, "Beware of suspicion. Suspicion is the most lying form of speech. Do not spy. Do not fight one another. Do not try to ensnare one another in sales. Do not hate one another. Be slaves of Allaah and brothers."
(Authenticated by Sheikh Al-Albaanee in Saheeh 'Adab al-Mufrad: 972)

Notes

Ibraaheem an-Nakhai'ee said, "Our companions used to allow us as young ones, all sorts of play things except for dogs."
(Authenticated by Sheikh Al-Albaanee in Saheeh 'Adab al-Mufrad: 976)

Muharram
7th

Notes

Muharram 8th

'Umar Ibn al-Khattab narrated that the Messenger of Allaah, may Allaah's praise and salutations be upon him said, "Whoever makes wudhu, performing it well, and then says, 'I bear witness that none has the right to be worshipped except Allaah, alone, without any partners, and I bear witness that Muhammad is His slave and Messenger. Oh Allaah, make me of those who return to You often in repentance and make me of those who remain clean and pure.' Then the eight gates of Paradise are opened for him, that he may enter by whichever of them he wishes." (Sunan at-Tirmidhee:55 -Authenticated by Sheikh al-Albaanee)

Notes

"A man asked 'Abdullah Ibn 'Amr Ibn al-'Aas, saying, 'Which of the Believers is best in his Islaam?' He replied, 'He from whose tongue and hand the Muslims are safe.' He asked, 'Then what is the best jihaad?' He replied, 'He who strives against his own self and desires for Allaah.' He asked, 'Then which of those who makes hijrah is best?' He replied, 'He who strives against his own self and desires for the sake of Allaah.' He asked, 'Is it something you have said, Oh 'Abdullah Ibn 'Amr, or Allaah's Messenger, may Allaah's praise and salutations be upon him?' He said, 'Rather, Allaah's Messenger, may Allaah's praise and salutations be upon him, said it."
(Authentically reported by Ibn Nasr al-Marwazee in Ta'zeem Qadris Salaat: 639)

Notes

Muharram
10th

Bakr al-Mazanee said, "When the tribulation of Ibn Al-Ashath occurred, Talq Ibn Habeeb said, 'Guard against this trial through taqwa.' It was said to him, 'Describe the fear of Allaah for us.' He said, 'Acting in obedience to Allaah upon a light from Him, hoping for Allaah's reward. And with this, turning away from acts of disobedience to Allaah, upon a light from Him, fearing His punishment.' Imaam ad-Dhahaabee said, 'In this statement he has spoken concisely and excellently, as there is no fearing of Allaah except through one's actions, and such actions do not come forth except through forethought, which itself comes from knowledge and submission to guidance. And none of this benefits except when it is established upon sincerity for the sake of Allaah alone. It is not said that so and so has left transgressing due to the light of comprehending such and such matter, as then the transgressor would require understanding of it to distance himself from it. Rather, his truly turning away from it comes from the fear of Allaah, not due to being praised for leaving it. Certainly the one who adheres to this advice will be successful." (Siyaar 'Alaam an-Nubala: vol. 4, page 601)

Notes

Sa'id al-Maqburi said, "I passed by Ibn 'Umar who had a man with him with whom he was conversing. I went to them, and he struck me on the chest and said, 'When you find two men conversing, do not go up to them nor sit with them until they give you permission.' I said. 'May Allaah make you prosper, Abu 'AbdurRahman. I hoped that I would hear something good from you.'"
(Authenticated by Sheikh Al-Albaanee in Saheeh 'Adab al-Mufrad: 889)

11th

Notes

Muharram
12th

"Oh you who believe! Stand out firmly for justice, as witnesses to Allaah, even though it be against yourselves, or your parents, or your kin, be he rich or poor; Allaah is a Better Protector to both (than you). So follow not the lusts of your hearts, lest you avoid justice; and if you distort your witness or refuse to give it, verily, Allaah is Ever Well-Acquainted with what you do. "
(Surah an-Nisaa:135)

Notes

Sahl narrated: I heard the Prophet saying, "A small place equal to an area occupied by a whip in Paradise is better than the whole world and whatever is in it; and undertaking a journey in the forenoon or in the afternoon for Allaah's Cause is better than the whole world and whatever is in it."
(Saheeh al-Bukhaaree: 6415)

Notes

Muharram
14th

"Oh mankind! There has come to you a good advice from your Lord- the Qur'an, and a healing for that which is in your breasts, a guidance and a mercy for the believers (Surah Yoonus:57)

Notes

"The believer is a mirror for the believer, and the believer is the brother of the believer. He safeguards his property for him and defends him from behind" (Authentically reported by Imam al-Bukharee in al- Adabul Mufrad:239, Sunan Abu Dawood: 4900)

Notes

Muharram 16th

'Oh Allaah, forgive me all of my sins, the small and great of them, the first and last of them, and the apparent and the hidden of them.'
(Collected in Sunan Abu Dawud 1 230-Authenticated by Sheikh Al-Albaanee)

Notes

Ibn 'Abbas reported that the Prophet, may Allaah's praise and salutations be upon him, said, "Whoever fashions an image will have to breathe life into it and he will be punished since he will not be able to breathe life into it. Anyone who claims to have seen a vision in a dream will have to string two beads of barley together and he will be punished because he will not be able to string them together. Anyone who listens to people's conversation when they move away from him will have molten lead poured into his ears."
(Authenticated by Sheikh Al-Albaanee in Saheeh 'Adab al-Mufrad: 883)

Notes

Muharram 18th

'Oh Allaah, I take refuge within Your pleasure from Your displeasure and within Your pardon from Your punishment, and I take refuge in You from You. I cannot enumerate Your praise, You are as You have praised Yourself.'
(Saheeh Muslim 1 352)

Notes

Hasan al-Basree, may Allaah have mercy upon him said, "Accuse and blame your desires and opinions in light of the revealed religion of Allaah. Advise yourselves and your practice of the religion with the guidance of the Book of Allaah."   (Authentically reported in Al-Madkhal Ilaa as-Sunan al-Kubra: Chapter- What has been Mentioned concerning Censuring of Opinion and Undertaking the Use of Analogy when there Exists a Relevant Source Text, No. 159)

Notes

Muharram

20th

Shuayb Ibn Harb said, "I was with Zuhayr Ibn Mua'weeyah in Basrah, and he said to me, 'Oh Shuayb, I will not write down any hadeeth narrations except that I have the correct intention.' So we stayed at Basrah but we only wrote down a single hadeeth." (Siyaar 'Alaam an-Nubala: vol. 8, page 182)

Notes

Muhammad Ibn al-Hanafiyya said, "Unwise is the one who does not deal wisely with a person whose company he cannot avoid until Allaah decrees for him an exit from this or a way out."
(Authenticated by Sheikh Al-Albaanee in Saheeh 'Adab al-Mufrad:682)

Notes

Muharram
22nd

'Ali said, "'Ammar asked for permission to enter to visit the Prophet, may Allaah's praise and salutations be upon him, and the Prophet recognized his voice and said, 'Welcome with the best and purest greeting!'"
(Authenticated by Sheikh Al-Albaanee in Saheeh 'Adab al-Mufrad: 786)

Notes

Mother of the Believers Umm Salamah narrated: "The Messenger of Allaah, may Allaah's praise and salutations be upon him, never went out of my house without raising his eye to the sky and saying, 'Oh Allaah! I seek refuge in You lest I stray or be led astray, or slip or be made to slip, or oppress or be oppressed, or behave foolishly or be treated foolishly.'

(Sunan Abu Dawud: 5075, Sunan Ibn Maajah: 3884 and it has been authenticated by Sheikh al-Albaanee)

Muharram 23rd

Notes

"This Day shall every person be recompensed for what he earned. This Day no injustice shall be done to anybody. Truly, Allaah is Swift in reckoning. And warn them of the Day of Resurrection that is drawing near, when the hearts will be choking the throats, and they can neither return their hearts to their chests nor can they throw them out. There will be no friend, nor an intercessor for the wrongdoers, who could be given heed to. Allaah knows the fraud of the eyes, and all that the breasts conceal." (Surah Ghaafir: 017)

Notes

'Abdullah Ibn Masu'd narrated: "The Prophet drew a square and then drew a line in the middle of it and let it extend outside the square, and then drew several small lines attached to that central line, and said, 'This is the human being, and this, the square, is his lease of life, it encircles him from all sides or has encircled him. And this line, which is outside the square, is his hope, and these small lines are the calamities and troubles which may befall him- and if one misses him, another will overtake him, and if the other misses him, a third will overtake him." (Saheeh al-Bukhaaree: 6417)

Notes

Muharram

26th

'Amr Ibn al-'As said, "I am astonished at a man who flees from Allaah's decree when he is all the time attacking it, and who sees the speck in his brother's eye and not the larger fragment in his own eye. He exposes the grudge held in his brother's heart but not the one within himself. I have never entrusted anyone with a secret of mine and then blamed him for divulging it. How could I blame him when I have given him something he is incapable of fulfilling?" (Authenticated by Sheikh Al-Albaanee in Saheeh 'Adab al-Mufrad: 681)

Notes

Muharram
27th

"And who is better in speech than he who invites to Allaah, does righteous deeds and says, I am one of the Muslims. (Surah Fussilat:33). Al-Hasan al-Basree said explaining this verse, "This is the beloved of Allaah, this is the close friend of Allaah, this is the chosen one of Allaah, this is the most beloved of the all the people of earth to Allaah. He responded to the call of Allaah and called mankind to that to which he had responded. He did righteous deeds in response to it and said, `I am one of the Muslims.' This is Allaah's khaleefah." (Authentically reported in Tafseer Ibn Katheer)

Notes

43

Muharram

28th

Anas Ibn Maalik said that the Messenger of Allaah, may Allaah's praise and salutations be upon him, said, "The one who sends "salat" upon me a single time, Allaah sends "salat" upon him ten times, and removes from him ten mistakes, and raises him ten degrees." (Authenticated by Sheikh al-Albaanee in Saheeh al-Jaam'ea: 6259 & Sheikh Muqbil in al-Saheeh al-Musnad: 119)

Notes

Ubayy Ibn Ka'b said, "Adhere to the sabeel (the way) and Sunnah –he who remembers the Most-Merciful and his eyes swell up with tears due to the fear of Allaah except that he will never be touched by the fire. Indeed moderation in the sabeel and Sunnah is better than exertion in opposition to it."
(Authentically narrate by Imaam Ahmad in az-Zuhd)

Notes

Ibraaheem Ibn Faatek said, "I heard Abu Ya'qoob say, 'This world is an ocean, the Hereafter is that distant shore, the boat to be traveled within is fear of Allaah, and the people are the travelers within it.'"
(Siyaar 'Alaam an-Nubala: vol. 15, page 282)

Notes

...an extra journal page

Muharram

Notes

Safar

1438
NOV 2016

Yaum al-Sabt Saturday	Yaum al-Ahad Sunday	Yaum al-Ithnayn Monday	Yaum ath-Thulatha Tuesday	Yaum al-Arbi'a Wednesday	Yaum al-Khamees Thursday	Yaum al-Jumi'ah Friday
			1 1	2 2	3 3	4 4
5 5	6 6	7 7	8 8	9 9	10 10	11 11
12 12	13 13	14 14	15 15	16 16	17 17	18 18
19 19	20 20	21 21	22 22	23 23	24 24	25 25
26 26	27 27	28 28	30 30			

"...Then He ordained that they eat from His provisions which He placed there for them. He made it subservient to them, and made it level and even, and placed within it pathways and routes for them to travel within it, and placed on this earth their sustenance. And Allaah mentions the arrangement of this earth as a place of habitation for them to utilize and travel through it, going here and returning from there, eating what is found within it for the one residing there. Yet He then concluded the verse with a clear reminder in His statement, "...and to Him will be the Resurrection." (Surah al-Mulk: 15) indicating that we will not remain in this present abode, nor stay here. Rather we entered it only as travelers upon a path; so it is not suitable that we take it as our permanent homeland or a place where we will in fact remain. But we only entered it in order to take from it that needed provision for the Hereafter- so it is actually only a place of transition, not one of permanent enjoyment; it is only a crossing point and passageway, not a permanent home and settlement."

(Sheikh al-Islaam Ibn Qayyim in his work "al-Fawaid", page 18)

Allaah, this is the close friend of Allaah, this is the chosen one of Allaah, this is the most beloved of the all the people of earth to Allaah. He responded to the call of Allaah and called mankind to that to which he had responded. He did righteous deeds in response to it and said, `I am one of the Muslims.' This is Allaah's khaleefah."
(Authentically reported in Tafseer Ibn Katheer)

Safar
1st

Notes

Ibraaheem Ibn Faatek said, "I heard Abu Ya'qoob say, 'This world is an ocean, the Hereafter is that distant shore, the boat to be traveled within is fear of Allaah, and the people are the travelers within it.'"
(Siyaar 'Alaam an-Nubala: vol. 15, page 282)

Notes

Nafi' said, "Ibn 'Umar used to strike his son for making grammatical mistakes."
(Authenticated by Sheikh Al-Albaanee in Saheeh 'Adab al-Mufrad: 676)

Notes

Safar

4th

"And We certainly sent into every nation a messenger, saying], "Worship Allah and avoid Taghut." And among them were those whom Allah guided, and among them were those upon whom error was deservedly decreed. So proceed through the earth and observe how was the end of the deniers." -(Surah Nahl: 36)

Notes

'Abdur-Rahman Ibn Mahdee said, "I used to attend a gathering on the day of Juma'ah, and if many people came I was pleased, and if few came I was saddened. So I asked Bishr Ibn Mansoor about this feeling, and he said to me, 'This is an evil gathering, do not return to it.' So I did not return to it."
(Siyaar 'Alaam an-Nubala: vol. 9, page 196)

Notes

Narrated By Anas Ibn Maalik: The Prophet, may Allaah's praise and salutations be upon him, said, 'When a man goes out of his house and says, "In the name of Allaah, I trust in Allaah; there is no might and no power but in Allaah," the following will be said to him at that time: "You are guided, defended and protected." The shaytaans will go far away from him and another shaytaan will say: "How can you deal with a man who has been guided, defended and protected?"'"

(Sunan Abu Dawud: 5097, Sunan at-Tirmidhee: 3426 and it has been authenticated by Sheikh al-Albaanee)

Notes

Ibn Mas'ud was heard to say, "You are living at a time when there are many men of understanding and few speakers. There are few who ask and many who give. In it there is more action than diversion. After you, there will come a time when there are few men of understanding and many speakers. There will be many who ask and few who give, while desires becomes what directs people's deeds. Know that right guidance at the end of time is better than some other actions."

(Authenticated by Sheikh Al-Albaanee in Saheeh 'Adab al-Mufrad: 605)

Notes

Safar

8th

And He has also sent to you a Messenger who recites to you the Verses of Allaah containing clear explanations, that He may take out those who believe and do righteous good deeds from the darkness of associating others with Allaah and disbelief into the light of worshiping Him alone. And whosoever believes in Allaah and performs righteous good deeds, He will admit him into Gardens under which rivers flow, to dwell therein forever. Allaah has indeed granted for him an excellent provision." (Surah at-Talaaq: 11)

Notes

Narrated 'Uqba Ibn 'Amir: "The Prophet went out and offered the funeral prayer for the martyrs of the battle of Uhud and then ascended the pulpit and said, 'I am your predecessor and I am a witness against you. By Allaah, I am now looking at my pool -Al-Kauthar-and I have been given the keys of the treasures of the earth (or the keys of the earth). By Allaah! I am not afraid that after me you will worship others besides Allaah, but I am afraid that you will start competing for the pleasures of this world.'" (Saheeh al-Bukhaaree: 6226)

Safar
9th

Notes

Safar
10th

Anas reported that the Prophet, may Allaah's praise and salutations be upon him, saw a man driving a sacrificial camel instead of riding it. "Ride it," he told him. The man replied, "It is a sacrificial camel." "Ride it," he repeated. The man said again, "It is a sacrificial camel." "Ride it," he repeated. The man said, "It is a sacrificial camel." The Prophet said, "Ride it, what's wrong with you!" (Authenticated by Sheikh Al-Albaanee in Saheeh 'Adab al-Mufrad:)

Notes

'Adi Ibn Arta' said, "When one of the Companions of the Prophet, may Allaah's praise and salutations be upon him, was praised, he said (in supplication to Allaah), 'Do not take me to task for what they say and forgive me for what they do not know.'"
(Authenticated by Sheikh Al-Albaanee in Saheeh 'Adab al-Mufrad: 585)

Notes

"By Al-'Asr (the time). Verily man is in loss. Except those who believe, do righteous good deeds, and recommend one another to the truth and recommend one another to patience. (Surah al-Asr:1-3). Ibn Qayyim said, "And an explanation of this is that by the completion and perfection of the four levels, an individual attains the upper limit in his perfection. The first: Knowing the truth; the second: acting upon it; the third: teaching it to the one who is not conversant with it; and the fourth: having patience in learning it, acting upon it and teaching it." (Miftaah Daarus-Sa'aadah 1 61)

Notes

"Jibreel came to me and said, 'Oh Muhammad! Live as you will for you must certainly die; love whom you will since you must certainly leave him; act as you will since you will certainly be given due reward for it; know that the believer's eminence is his standing in prayer during the night, and his honor is having sufficiency without dependency upon the people.'"
(Authentically narrated Silsilaat al-Hadeeth as-Saheehah: 831)

Notes

Safar 14th

Al-Khareebe said, "We use to consider it preferable to be like a man who strove in concealing his good works, without informing his wife or others about them." (Siyaar 'Alaam an-Nubala: vol. 9, page 349)

Notes

Abu Hurairah reported that the Messenger of Allaah, may Allaah's praise and salutations be upon him, said, "When you hear a man saying, 'People are destroyed,' then he himself has destroyed them."
(Authenticated by Sheikh Al-Albaanee in Saheeh 'Adab al-Mufrad: 583)

Safar
15th

Notes

"So, as for those who believed and did deeds of righteousness, He will give them their due rewards – and more out of His bounty. But as for those who refused His worship and were proud, He will punish them with a painful torment. And they will not find for themselves besides Allaah any protector or helper. Oh mankind! Verily, there has come to you a convincing proof from your Lord; and We sent down to you a manifest light." (Surah an-Nisaa:173)

Notes

Sahl Ibn Sa'd narrated: "I heard Ibn Az-Zubair who was on the pulpit at Mecca, delivering a sermon, saying, 'Oh men! The Prophet used to say, "If the son of Adam were given a valley full of gold, he would love to have a second one; and if he were given the second one, he would love to have a third, for nothing fills the belly of Adam's son except dust. And Allaah forgives he who repents to Him." Ubai said, "We considered this as a saying from the Qur'an till the Surah beginning with 'The mutual rivalry for piling up of worldly things diverts you..' (102.1) was revealed.'" (Saheeh al-Bukhaaree: 6438)

Safar
17th

Notes

Safar

18th

"And say, 'Oh Lord! Increase me in knowledge...'" (Surah Taa Haa: 114).

Notes

Sa'd Ibn Abi Waqqas transmitted that the Prophet, may Allaah's praise and salutations be upon him, said to him, "You do not spend anything by which you desire the face of Allaah Almighty but that you are rewarded for it, even that which you place in your wife's mouth."
(Authenticated by Sheikh Al-Albaanee in Saheeh 'Adab al-Mufrad: 579)

Safar
19th

Notes

Safar

20th

And the Messenger used to say, "Oh Allaah, benefit me with that which you have taught me, and teach me that which will benefit me, and increase me in knowledge. (Authentically reported in Sunan Ibn Maajah (1 47)).

Notes

"And don't be weak in the pursuit of the enemy. If you are suffering hardships then surely they too are suffering hardships as you are suffering- but you have a hope from Allaah for the reward of Paradise, for which they hope not; and Allaah is Ever All-Knowing, All-Wise." (Surah an-Nisaa:104)

Notes

Sulaymaan al-Haashamee said, "Sometimes I would narrate a single hadeeth narration having a clear intention for Allaah, then I would come upon some people to narrate the hadeeth and my intention would have changed. So even a single hadeeth requires making more than one correct intention for it." (Siyaar 'Alaam an-Nubala: vol. 10, page 625)

Notes

Thawban reported that the Prophet, may Allaah's praise and salutations be upon him, said, "The best dinar a man spends is the dinar which he spends on his family, the dinar which he spends on his companions in the way of Allaah, and the dinar which he spends on his riding animal in the way of Allaah." One of the transmitters, Abu Qilaba, said, "He began with the family. Who has a greater reward that the man who spends on small children until such time that Allaah Almighty makes them able to support themselves?"

(Authenticated by Sheikh Al-Albaanee in Saheeh 'Adab al-Mufrad: 575)

Notes

Safar 24th

Allaah's Messenger explained this to his Companions, thus: One day he drew a straight line for them on the ground and then drew many short lines on both sides of it. He then recited the previous verse whilst he was moving his noble finger over the straight line, and he said, "This is Allaah's Path." He then pointed to the other lines and said, "These are other paths, and at the head of each one there is a shaytaan calling towards it." (Authenticated by Sheikh al-Albaanee in Dhilaalul-Jannah fee Takhreejus-Sunnah: no.16)

Notes

Talq Ibn Habeeb said, "Indeed the rights of Allaah are greater than can be properly established by the worshipers of Allaah, and the blessings of Allaah are more numerous than can be counted, so approach the morning as those making repentance, and enter the evening as those making repentance." (Siyaar 'Alaam an-Nubala: vol. 4, page 602)

Notes

Safar

26th

Narrated Zahdam Ibn Mudarrib: 'Imran Ibn Husain said: "The Prophet said, 'The best people are my generation and then those who come after them of the next generation.'" Imran added, "I am not sure whether the Prophet repeated the statement twice after his first saying of it. The Prophet added, 'And after them there will come people who will bear witness, though they will not be asked to give their witness; and they will be treacherous and nobody will trust them, and they will make vows, but will not fulfill them, and fatness will appear among them.'" (Saheeh al-Bukhaaree)

Notes

'Oh Allaah, I have indeed oppressed my soul excessively and none can forgive sin except You, so forgive me a forgiveness from Yourself and have mercy upon me. Surely, You are The Most-Forgiving, The Most-Merciful.'
(Collected in Saheeh al-Bukhaaree 8 168 and Saheeh Muslim 4 2078)

Safar
27th

Notes

Safar

28th

'Oh Allaah, forgive me for those sins which have come to pass as well as those which shall occur in the future, and those I have committed in secret as well as those I have made public, and those wherein I have exceeded all bounds as well as those things about which You are more knowledgeable. You are Al-Muqaddim and Al-Muakhkhir. None has the right to be worshipped except You.' (Collected in Saheeh Muslim 1 534)

Notes

Abu Hurairah reported that the Prophet, may Allaah's praise and salutations be upon him, said, "No believer turns his face to Allaah and asks Him for something but that He gives it to him, either by giving it to him sooner in this world or storing it up for him in the Next World, as long as he does not try to make it come quickly." They asked, "Messenger of Allaah, what does 'making it come quickly' mean?" He said, "That he says, 'I asked and asked and do not think that I will be answered.'"

(Authenticated by Sheikh Al-Albaanee in Saheeh 'Adab al-Mufrad: 548)

Safar
29th

Notes

Narrated Mujaahid: 'Abdullah Ibn 'Umar said, "Allaah's Messenger took hold of my shoulder and said, 'Be in this world as if you were a stranger or a traveler." The sub-narrator added, Ibn 'Umar used to say, "If you survive till the evening, do not expect to be alive in the morning, and if you survive till the morning, do not expect to be alive in the evening, and take from your health for your sickness, and take from your life for your death." (Saheeh al-Bukhaaree)

Notes

...an extra journal page

Notes

Rabee'a al-Awwal

1438

NOV / DEC 2016

Yaum as-Sabt Saturday	Yaum al-Ahad Sunday	Yaum al-Ithnayn Monday	Yaum ath-Thulatha Tuesday	Yaum al-Arbi'a Wednesday	Yaum al-Khamees Thursday	Yaum al-Jumu'ah Friday
				1 30	2 1	3 2
4 3	5 4	6 5	7 6	8 7	9 8	10 9
11 10	12 11	13 12	14 13	15 14	16 15	17 16
18 17	19 18	20 19	21 20	22 21	23 22	24 23
25 24	26 25	27 26	28 27	29 28	30 29	

"Similarly this applies to beliefs and whatever one wants and has an attachment to; as if the heart is filled with false beliefs and false love, then there is remains no place within it for the correct belief and proper love. Likewise the tongue- if it is preoccupied with talking about that which does not benefit it, then it is not possible for its owner to engage in speech that would benefit him until he clears his tongue from being engaged in that futile, fruitless speech. Indeed, the case is the same for the limbs of the body, as if they are similarly preoccupied with acts that are not those of obedience then it is not possible that at the same time they be engaged in acts of obedience, until they are truly cleared from their opposite."

(Sheikh al-Islaam Ibn Qayyim in his work *"al-Fawaid"*, page 29)

"Did you think that We had created you in play -without any purpose-, and that you would not be brought back to Us?"
(Surah al-Mu.minoon:115)

Rabee'a
al-Awwal
1st

Notes

Rifa'a az-Zurqi said, "In the Battle of Uhud when those who associated others with Allaah in worship retreated, the Messenger of Allaah, may Allaah's praise and salutations be upon him, said, 'Form straight ranks so that I can praise my Almighty Lord.' They formed in ranks behind him. He said, 'Oh Allaah, all praise is due to You. Oh Allaah, none can contract what You expand nor bring near what you put far away. None can put far away what You bring near. None can give what You withhold nor withhold what You give. Oh Allaah, expand to us some of Your blessings, mercy and favor and give us provision! Oh Allaah, I ask You for the abiding blessing which is neither changed nor removed. Oh Allaah, I ask You for blessing on the Day of Utter Poverty and security on the Day of Fear. Oh Allaah, I seek refuge with You from the evil of what You give us. Oh Allaah, make us love belief and adorn our hearts with it. Make us hate disbelief, deviance and rebellion. Place us among the rightly-guided. Oh Allaah, make us die as Muslims and make us live as Muslims and join us to the rightly acting, who are neither disappointed nor afflicted. Oh Allaah, fight the unbelievers who bar Your path and who deny Your Messengers. Place Your abasement and punishment over them. Oh Allaah, fight the unbelievers who were given the Book, Oh Lord of Truth!'"
(Authenticated by Sheikh Al-Albaanee in Saheeh 'Adab al-Mufrad: 538)

Notes

Hasan al-Basree said, "Oh son of Aadam, leaving a sin is easier upon you than remedying it through repentance."
(Siyaar 'Alaam an-Nubala: vol. 4, page 578)

Notes

Oh you who believe! When you go to fight in the Cause of Allaah, verify the truth, and say not to anyone who greets you (by embracing Islaam): "You are not a believer"; seeking the perishable goods of the worldly life. There are much more profits and booties with Allaah. Even as he is now, so were you yourselves before till Allaah conferred on you His Favors -guided you to Islaam, therefore, be cautious in discrimination. Allaah is Ever Well-Acquainted with what you do. (Surah an-Nisaa: 94)

Notes

Narrated Hakim Ibn Hizam: I asked the Prophet for some money and he gave it to me, and then again I asked him and he gave it to me, and then again I asked him and he gave me and he then said, "This wealth is like green and sweet fruit, and whoever takes it without greed, Allaah will bless it for him, but whoever takes it with greed, Allaah will not bless it for him, and he will be like the one who eats but is never satisfied. And the upper -giving- hand is better than the lower -taking- hand." (Saheeh al-Bukhaaree)

Notes

Oh you who believe! Enter perfectly into Islaam -by obeying all the rules and regulations of the religion of Islaam- and follow not the footsteps of Shaytaan. Verily, he is to you a plain enemy. (Surah al-Baqarah:208)

Abu Musa reported that the Prophet, may Allaah's praise and salutations be upon him, used to make this supplication: "Oh Allaah, forgive my errors, my ignorance and my excess in all my affairs, and what You know better than me of these things. Oh Allaah, forgive all my errors, what I do intentionally or out of my ignorance or in jest and in all that I do. Oh Allaah, forgive me my past and future wrong actions, what I conceal of them and what I divulge. You are the One who puts things ahead and the One who delays them. You have power over all things."

(Authenticated by Sheikh Al-Albaanee in Saheeh 'Adab al-Mufrad: 532)

Notes

Narrated 'Abdullah: The Prophet said, "Who among you considers the wealth of his heirs dearer to him than his own wealth?" They replied, "Oh Allaah's Messenger! There is none among us but loves his own wealth more." The Prophet said, "So his wealth is whatever he spends (in Allaah's Cause) during his life (in performance of good deeds) while the wealth of his heirs is whatever he leaves after his death."
(Saheeh al-Bukhaaree)

Notes

Rabee'a al-Awwal
8th

Shaqeeq al-Balkhee said, "The signs of repentance are that you cry for what you engaged in, have fear of falling into sins, abandon those previous evil companions, and hold fast to good companions."
(Siyaar 'Alaam an-Nubala: vol. 9, page 315)

Notes

"....The people proclaimed, 'We have believed in the Lord of the boy! We have believed in the Lord of the boy! We have believed in the Lord of the boy!' The king came, and it was said to him, 'That is the thing which you were afraid of. By Allaah! The thing which you were afraid of, has fallen upon you, the people have believed in Allaah.' So he ordered deep ditches to be dug at the entrances of the roads, and it was done, then fire was kindled in those ditches, and the king ordered that whoever did not abandon his religion be thrown into the ditches, and it was done. Then there came a woman with her baby. She nearly retreated back from the ditch but the baby said, 'Oh mother! Be patient, you are on the truth,' (So she threw herself in the ditch of the fire along with her child to be with the martyrs in Paradise)."
(Saheeh Muslim: 7148)

Notes

Anas said, "The Prophet, may Allaah's praise and salutations be upon him, most frequently said, "Oh Allaah, Oh Overturner of hearts, make my heart firm in Your deen."
(Authenticated by Sheikh Al-Albaanee in Saheeh 'Adab al-Mufrad: 527)

Notes

Sa'd Ibn Abee Waqaas said that the Messenger of Allaah, may Allaah's praise and salutations be upon him, said, "Four things are from contentedness: a righteous woman, a spacious home, a righteous neighbor, and a comfortable means of transport. And four things are from misery: a bad neighbor, a bad woman, a crowded home, and a poor means of transport.'

(Authenticated by Sheikh al-Albaanee in Silsilaat al-Hadeeth As-Saheehah: 282 & Sheikh Muqbil in al-Saheeh al-Musnad: 375)

Notes

Rabee'a al-Awwal

12th

Almighty Allaah says: "They, Jews and Christians, took their rabbis and their monks to be their lords besides Allaah, and they also took as their Lord Messiah, son of Maryam, while they were commanded to worship none but one Allaah, none has the right to be worshipped but He. Glorified is He, from having the partners they associate with Him." (Surah at-Tawbah: 31)

Notes

Once, while Messenger of Allaah, may Allaah's praise and salutations be upon him, was reciting the above verse, 'Adi Ibn Haatim said, "Oh Allaah's Prophet! They do not worship them, the rabbis and monks." The Messenger of Allaah, may Allaah's praise and salutations be upon him, said, "They certainly do. The rabbis and monks made legal things illegal, and illegal things legal, and they followed them, and by doing so they indeed worshipped them." (Authentically narrated by al-Musnad Ahmad, Sunan at-Tirmidhee, and others)

Rabee'a al-Awwal 13th

Notes

Notes

Notes

Once, while Messenger of Allaah, may Allaah's praise and salutations be upon him, was reciting the above verse, 'Adi Ibn Haatim said, "Oh Allaah's Prophet! They do not worship them, the rabbis and monks." The Messenger of Allaah, may Allaah's praise and salutations be upon him, said, "They certainly do. The rabbis and monks made legal things illegal, and illegal things legal, and they followed them, and by doing so they indeed worshipped them." (Authentically narrated by al-Musnad Ahmad, Sunan at-Tirmidhee, and others)

Rabee'a al-Awwal 13th

Notes

Once, while Messenger of Allaah, may Allaah's praise and salutations be upon him, was reciting the above verse, 'Adi Ibn Haatim said, "Oh Allaah's Prophet! They do not worship them, the rabbis and monks." The Messenger of Allaah, may Allaah's praise and salutations be upon him, said, "They certainly do. The rabbis and monks made legal things illegal, and illegal things legal, and they followed them, and by doing so they indeed worshipped them." (Authentically narrated by al-Musnad Ahmad, Sunan at-Tirmidhee, and others)

Rabee'a al-Awwal 13th

Notes

Bilaal Ibn Sa'd as-Sakoonee said, "Do not merely look at your small error, rather look at your overall disobedience of Allaah."
(Siyaar 'Alaam an-Nubala: vol. 5, page 91)

Notes

Jabir reported that the Messenger of Allaah, may Allaah's praise and salutations be upon him, said, "Oh Allaah, let my hearing and sight be sound and make them remain sound until I die. Turn away from me the one who wrongs me and give me revenge on him."
(Authenticated by Sheikh Al-Albaanee in Saheeh 'Adab al-Mufrad: 505)

Notes

"Oh my son! Establish the ritual prayers, enjoin on people what is right, and forbid people from wrongdoing, and bear with patience whatever befalls you. Verily, these are some of the important commandments ordered by Allaah with no exemption. And turn not your face away from men with pride, nor walk in insolence through the earth. Verily, Allaah likes not any arrogant boaster. And be moderate or show no insolence in your walking, and lower your voice. Verily, the harshest of all voices is the braying of the asses." (Surah Luqmaan:17-19)

Notes

"We sent a Messenger to every nation ordering them that they should worship Allaah alone, obey Him and make their worship purely for Him, and that they should avoid everything worshipped besides Allaah. So from them there were those whom Allaah guided to His religion, and there were those who were unbelievers for whom misguidance was ordained. So travel through the land and see the destruction that befell those who denied the Messengers and disbelieved. " –(Surah an-Nahl:36)

Notes

Jabir Ibn 'Abdullah reported that the Prophet, may Allaah's praise and salutations be upon him, went up the minbar. When he reached the first step, he said, "Ameen". When he ascended to the second step, he said, "Ameen," and when he stepped onto the third step, he said, "Ameen." They said, "Messenger of Allaah, we heard you say 'Ameen' three times." He said, "When I went up the first step, Jibreel, may Allaah's praise and salutations be upon him, came to me and said, 'Wretched is the worshiper to whom Ramadhaan comes and when it passes from him is not forgiven.' I said, 'Ameen.' Then he said, 'Wretched is the worshiper who has one or both of his parents alive and they do not let him enter the Garden.' I said, 'Ameen.' Then he said, 'Wretched is a worshiper who does not send salaams upon you when you are mentioned in his presence,' and I said, 'Ameen.'"

(Authenticated by Sheikh Al-Albaanee in Saheeh 'Adab al-Mufrad: 500)

Sufyaan at-Thawree said, "If there was someone with you who would then carry your statements to the ruler, would you talk about anything?" We said, "No". He then said, "Indeed there are with you those who carry up your statements (intending by this the angels)."
(Siyaar 'Alaam an-Nubala: vol. 7, page 267)

Rabee'a al-Awwal 19th

Notes

Narrated Abu Hurairah: He (the Messenger of Allaah, may Allaah's praise and salutations be upon him, said, "Oh Aba Hirr!" I said, "Labbaik, Oh Allaah's Messenger!" He said, "Go and call the people of Suffa to me."... The order of the Prophet upset me, and I said to myself, "How will this little milk be enough for the people of Suffa?", thinking that I was more entitled to drink from that milk in order to strengthen myself. But regardless (of what I thought) the Prophet had ordered me to give that milk to them. I wondered if any of that milk would be left for me?! But I could not do anything but obey Allaah and His Messenger so I went to the people of Suffa and called them....

...Finally, after the whole group had drunk their fill, I reached the Prophet,who took the bowl and put it on his hand, looked at me and smiled and said, "Oh Aba Hirr!" I replied, "Labbaik, Oh Allaah's Messenger!" He said, "There remain you and I." I said, "You have said the truth, Oh Allaah's Messenger!" He said, "Sit down and drink." I sat down and drank. He said, "Drink," and I drank. He kept on telling me repeatedly to drink, till I said, "No. by Allaah Who sent you with the Truth, I have no space for it in my stomach." He said, "Hand it over to me." When I gave him the bowl, he praised Allaah and pronounced Allaah's Name on it and drank the remaining milk. (Saheeh al-Bukhaaree)

Notes

Narrated Abu Hurairah: Allaah's Messenger said, "The deeds of anyone of you will not save you from the Hellfire." They said, "Even you will not be saved by your deeds, Oh Allaah's Messenger?" He said, "No, even I will not be saved unless and until Allaah bestows His Mercy upon me. Therefore, do good deeds properly, sincerely and moderately, and worship Allaah in the forenoon and in the afternoon and during a part of the night, and always adopt a middle, moderate, regular course whereby you will reach your goal of Paradise." (Saheeh al-Bukhaaree)

Notes

Narrated 'Aishah: Allaah's Messenger said, "Do good deeds properly, sincerely and moderately and know that your deeds will not make you enter Paradise, and that the most beloved deed to Allaah's is the most regular and constant even though it were little." (Saheeh al-Bukhaaree)

Notes

Umm Kulthum, the daughter of Abu Bakr, reported that 'Aishah said, "The Prophet, may Allaah's praise and salutations be upon him, came to me while I was praying when he needed something. I was taking a long time and he said, ''Aishah, you must make the comprehensive supplication.' When I finished, I asked, 'Messenger of Allaah, what is the comprehensive supplication?' He said, 'Say: "Oh Allaah, I ask You for all good, both sooner and later, what I know of it and what I do not know. I seek refuge with You from all evil, both sooner and later, what I know of it and what I do not know. I ask You for the Garden and whatever words or actions bring one near to it. I seek refuge with You from the Fire and whatever words or actions bring one near to it. I ask You by what Muhammad asked You and I seek refuge from You by what Muhammad sought refuge from and whatever fate You have decreed for me, make its end right guidance.'"
(Authenticated by Sheikh Al-Albaanee in Saheeh 'Adab al-Mufrad: 397)

Notes

"This day, those who disbelieved have given up all hope of your religion; so fear them not; but fear Me. This day, I have perfected your religion for you, completed My Favor upon you, and have chosen for you Islaam as your religion." –(Surah al-Maa'edah: 3)

Notes

"I have been sent before the Hour so that Allaah alone should be worshipped without any partner for Him, and my provision has been placed beneath the shade of my spear, and subservience and humiliation have been placed upon those who disobey my orders, and whoever imitates a people then he is one of them." (Authentically reported in al-Musnad by Ahmad: 5114)

Notes

Rabee'a al-Awwal

26th

Muhammad Ibn 'Abaas said, "From the signs of love of Allaah are controlling oneself for the sake of the beloved, and searching for that which pleases Him," (Siyaar 'Alaam an-Nubala: vol. 10, page 391)

Notes

A man came to the Prophet, may Allaah's praise and salutations be upon him, and said, "Messenger of Allaah, what is the best supplication?" He answered, "Asking Allaah for forgiveness and well-being in this world and the Hereafter." Then he came to him the following day and asked, "Prophet of Allaah, what is the best supplication?" He answered, "Asking Allaah for forgiveness and well-being in this world and the Hereafter. When you are given well-being in this world and the Hereafter, then you have achieved success."
(Authenticated by Sheikh Al-Albaanee in Saheeh 'Adab al-Mufrad: 495)

Notes

"Oh you who believe! Obey Allaah and obey the Messenger, and those of you Muslims who are in authority. And if you differ in anything amongst yourselves, refer it to Allaah and His Messenger, if you believe in Allaah and in the Last Day. That is better and more suitable for final determination."
(Surah an-Nisaa:059)

Notes

Narrated 'Aishah: The Prophet was asked, "What deeds are loved most by Allaah?" He said, "The most regular constant deeds even though they may be few." He added, 'Don't take upon yourselves, except the deeds which are within your ability." (Saheeh al-Bukhaaree: 472)

Notes

Narrated Abu Wail: We paid a visit to Khabbab who was sick, and he said, "We migrated with the Prophet for Allaah's Sake and our wages became due on Allaah to recompense us. Some of us died without having received anything of the wages, and one of them was Mus'ab Ibn 'Umar, who was martyred on the day of the battle of Uhud, leaving only one sheet to shroud him in. If we covered his head with it, his feet became uncovered, and if we covered his feet with it, his head became uncovered. So the Prophet ordered us to cover his head with it and put some Idhkhir -a kind of grass- over his feet. Whereas on the other hand, some of us have had the fruits of our good deeds and are harvesting them in this world." (Saheeh al-Bukhaaree)

Notes

...an extra journal page

Notes

Rabee'a ath-Thaanee

1438

DEC/ JAN 2017

Yawn al-Sabt Saturday	Yawn al-Ahad Sunday	Yawn al-Ithnayn Monday	Yawn ath-Thulatha Tuesday	Yawn al-Arbi'a Wednesday	Yawn al-Khamees Thursday	Yawn al-Jumi'ah Friday
						1 30
2 31	3 1	4 2	5 3	6 4	7 5	8 6
9 7	10 8	11 9	12 10	13 11	14 12	15 13
16 14	17 15	18 16	19 17	20 18	21 19	22 20
23 21	24 22	25 23	26 24	27 25	28 26	29 27
30 28						

"-The people of this world are firstly like a servant who has a master that he will soon stand before to be responsible for what he has completed of his duties, and secondly like someone who has a house that he will soon have to go live in. So it is necessary that everyone engage in that which will please his master before that accounting, and that one prepares furnishings for his future home before he arrives.

-The wasting of time is something worse than death, as the wasting of time cuts you off from what Allaah is pleased with and the possible rewards in the next life, whereas death only cuts you off from this passing world and its people.

-The present world, from its beginning to its end, is not even worth someone's suffering an hour of sadness, so how could it be worth someone suffering for an entire lifetime?!'"

(Sheikh al-Islaam Ibn Qayyim in his work *"al-Fawaid"*, page 31)

Abu Alee at-Thaqafee said: Abu Hafs used to say, "The one who does not each moment weigh his situation and condition against the scale of the Book of Allaah and the Sunnah, and does not question his very footsteps, then he is not to be considered worthy." (Siyaar 'Alaam an-Nubala: vol. 12, 512)

Rabee'a ath-Thaanee 1st

Notes

Rabee'a ath-Thaanee

2nd

It is related that 'Abdullah used to use these supplications often: "Our Lord, make peace between us and guide us on the path of Islaam. Save us from the darkness and bring us to the light. Remove acts of deviance from us, both open and hidden. Bless us in our ears, our eyes, our hearts, our wives and our children. Turn to us. You are the Ever-Turning, Most Merciful. Make us thankful for Your blessing and make us among those who give praise for it and proclaim it. Perfect it is for us." (Authenticated by Sheikh Al-Albaanee in Saheeh 'Adab al-Mufrad: 490)

Notes

And indeed We bestowed upon Luqmaan Al-Hikmah, wisdom and religious understanding, saying: "Give thanks to Allaah." And whoever gives thanks, he gives thanks for the good of his own self. And whoever is unthankful, then verily, Allaah is All-Rich, Free of all needs, Worthy of all praise. And remember when Luqmaan said to his son when he was advising him: "Oh my son! Join not in worship others with Allaah. Verily, joining others in worship with Allaah is a great wrongdoing indeed. (Surah Luqmaan:12-13)

Narrated Abu Hurairah: Allaah's Messenger said, "Whoever believes in Allaah and the Last Day should speak what is good or keep quiet, and whoever believes in Allaah and the Last Day should not hurt (or insult) his neighbor; and whoever believes in Allaah and the Last Day should entertain his guest generously." (Saheeh al-Bukhaaree)

Notes

"Oh Prophet! When believing women come to you to give you the pledge of allegiance, that they will not associate anything in worship with Allaah, that they will not steal, that they will not commit illegal sexual intercourse, that they will not kill their children, that they will not utter slander, intentionally forging falsehood by attributing illegal children to their husbands, and that they will not disobey you in all that which Islaam ordains, then accept their pledge of allegiance, and ask Allaah to forgive them. Verily, Allaah is Oft-Forgiving, Most Merciful. Oh you who believe! Take not as friends the people who incurred the Wrath of Allaah, the Jews. Surely, they have despaired of receiving any good in the Hereafter, just as the disbelievers have despaired of those buried in graves that they will not be resurrected on the Day of Resurrection. (Surah al-Mumtahanah:12-13)

Notes

Abu Bakr as-Sadeeq was heard to say, "The supplication of one's brother in Allaah is answered."
(Authenticated by Sheikh Al-Albaanee in Saheeh 'Adab al-Mufrad: 486)

Notes

"Richness is not having many belongings, but richness is contentment of the soul." (Saheeh Muslim: 2287)

"When you understand this introduction, then you will realize that perfect pleasure, rejoicing, happiness, a good life and bliss - all lies in having knowledge of Allaah, worshiping Him alone and being content with Him, being eager to meet with Him, gathering one's heart, attention, and concerns all upon Him. For the truly difficult life is the life of the one whose heart is scattered in focus, and whose priorities are divided diverse. As then there is no firm focus which his heart can settle upon nor any single beloved in whom he can turn to and find solace with..."

(A Treatise Written by Ibn Qayyim to One of His Brothers, page 32-33)

An-Nu'man Ibn Bashir was heard to say on the minbar, "Shaytaan has snares and traps. From the snares and traps of Shaytaan are to gloat ungratefully in the blessings of Allaah, to boast about the gifts of Allaah, to have pride at the expense of other worshippers of Allaah, and to follow one's desire for other than the sake of Allaah."

(Authenticated by Sheikh Al-Albaanee in Saheeh 'Adab al-Mufrad: 430)

Notes

"He who obeys the Messenger, has indeed obeyed Allaah, but he who turns away, then We have not sent you as a watcher over them. They say, "We are obedient," but when they leave you, a section of them spends all night in planning other than what you say. But Allaah records their nightly plots. So turn aside from them, do not punish them, and put your trust in Allaah. And Allaah is Ever All-Sufficient as a Disposer of affairs. Do they not then consider the Qur'an carefully? Had it been from other than Allaah, they would surely have found therein many a contradiction. (Surah an-Nisaa:80-82)

Notes

Narrated Al-Mughira Ibn Shu'ba: "The Prophet used to pray so much that his feet used to become swollen, and when he was asked as to why he prayed so much, he would say, "Shall I not be a thankful slave to Allaah?"
(Saheeh al-Bukhaaree)

Notes

Abdullah Ibn Abi al-Hudhayl said, "'Abdullah Ibn Mas'ud went to visit a sick person with some other people. There was a woman in the room and one of the men began to look at her. 'Abdullah said to him, 'It would have been better for you if your eyes had been gouged out than that you do this.'"
(Authenticated by Sheikh Al-Albaanee in Saheeh 'Adab al-Mufrad: 412)

Notes

"And they said, "If it had been the will of the Most Gracious, we should not have worshipped these false deities." They have no knowledge whatsoever of that. They do nothing but lie. Or have We given them any Book before this -the Qur'an- to which they are holding fast? No! They say: "We found our fathers following a certain way and religion, and we guide ourselves by their footsteps." (Surah az-Zukhruf:20-22)

Notes

Al-Hukm Ibn 'Amr al-Ghafaaree said, "I swear by Allaah, if the heavens and earth were to surround and close in upon a worshiper of Allaah, through the worshiper's fear of Allaah, Allaah would make between them a way out for him." (Siyaar 'Alaam an-Nubala: vol. 2, page 475)

Notes

Abu Sa'id al-Khudri reported that he came to the Messenger of Allaah, may Allaah's praise and salutations be upon him, while he had a fever. He had a covering over him. He placed his hand on him and discovered that it was hot above the covering. Abu Sa'id exclaimed, 'How hot your fever is, Messenger of Allaah!' He said, 'We are like that. The affliction is hard on us, but the reward is doubled for us.' He said, 'Messenger of Allaah, which people have the greatest affliction?' He replied, 'The Prophets, and then the righteous. One of them was tested by poverty to such an extent that he could only find a robe to cover himself with and so he wore that. Another was tested by fleas until they killed him. They had greater joy in receiving affliction than one of you has in receiving favors.'"
(Authenticated by Sheikh Al-Albaanee in Saheeh 'Adab al-Mufrad: 395)

Notes

"And similarly, We sent not a warner before you to any town of people but the luxurious ones among them said, "We found our fathers following a certain way and religion, and we will indeed follow their footsteps." The warner said, "Even if I bring you better guidance than that which you found your fathers following?" They said, "Verily, we disbelieve in that with which you have been sent." (Surah az-Zukhruf:23-24)

Notes

Narrated Abu Hurairah: The Prophet said, "A worshiper may utter a word which pleases Allaah without giving it much importance, and because of that Allaah will raise him to degrees of reward; or a worshiper may utter a word carelessly which displeases Allaah without thinking of its gravity and because of that he will be thrown into the Hell-Fire." (Saheeh al-Bukhaaree)

Notes

Abu Hurairah reported that the Prophet, may Allaah's praise and salutations be upon him, said, "Affliction will continue to trouble the believers, men and women, in their bodies, their families, and their property until they meet Allaah Almighty purified of every wrong action."
(Authenticated by Sheikh Al-Albaanee in Saheeh 'Adab al-Mufrad: 380)

Notes

"... I said, "Hanzalah is guilty of hypocrisy Oh Messenger of Allaah." So the Messenger of Allaah, may Allaah's praise and salutations be upon him, said, "And how is that?" I said, "When we are with you, you remind us of the Fire and of Paradise and it is as if we are seeing it with our own eyes. Then when we depart from you and attend our wives, our children and our business then much of this slips from our minds." So the Messenger of Allaah, may Allaah's praise and salutations be upon him, said, "By Him in whose hand is my soul- if you remained continually as you are when you are with me and in remembering Allaah then the angels would shake hands with you upon your beds and upon your roads. But Oh Hanzalah, there is a time for this and a time for that, there is a time for this and a time for that, there is a time for this and a time for that." (Saheeh Muslim: 6223)

Notes

Khaalid Ibn Ma'daan said, "If one of you has a door of good opened up for him, then you should hurry to pass through, as you do not know when it may close." (Siyaar 'Alaam an-Nubala: vol. 4, page 540)

Abu Hurairah reported that the Prophet, may Allaah's praise and salutations be upon him, said, "A Muslim does not encounter fatigue, tiredness, concern, sorrow, injury or grief, or even a thorn which pricks him, without Allaah expiating his errors for him by that."
(Authenticated by Sheikh Al-Albaanee in Saheeh 'Adab al-Mufrad: 378)

Rabee'a ath-Thaanee

21st

Notes

133

"And whosoever turns away blindly from the remembrance of the Most Gracious, We appoint for him a shaytaan to be a companion to him. And verily, they, the shaytaans, hinder them from the path of Allaah, but they think that they are guided aright!" (Surah az-Zukhruf:36-47)

Notes

Narrated Abu Hurairah: I heard Allaah's Messenger, may Allaah's praise and salutations be upon him, saying, "My example and the example of the people is that of a man who made a fire, and when it lighted what was around it, moths and other insects started falling into the fire. The man tried his best to prevent them from falling into the fire, but they overpowered him and rushed into the fire." The Prophet added, "Now, similarly, I take hold of the knots at your waist belts to prevent you from falling into the Fire, but you insist on falling into it." (Saheeh al-Bukhaaree)

Notes

Anas Ibn Malik reported that the Prophet, may Allaah's praise and salutations be upon him, said, "If the Final Hour arrives while you have a palm seedling in your hands and it is possible to plant it before the Hour comes, you should go ahead and plant it."
(Authenticated by Sheikh Al-Albaanee in Saheeh 'Adab al-Mufrad: 371)

Notes

"On the Day you shall see the believing men and the believing women, their light running forward before them and with their Records -Books of deeds- in their right hands. Glad tidings for you this Day! Gardens under which rivers flow, to dwell therein forever! Truly, this is the great success! On the Day when the hypocrites – men and women – will say to the believers, "Wait for us! Let us get something from your light!" It will be said, "Go back to your rear! Then seek a light!" So, a wall will be put up between them, with a gate therein. Inside it will be mercy, and outside it will be torment." (Surah al-Hadeed:12-13)

Notes

The Messenger of Allaah, may Allaah's praise and salutations be upon him, said, "A group of people amongst my Ummah will remain obedient to Allaah's orders. They will not be harmed by those who leave them nor by those who oppose them, until Allaah's command for the Last Day comes upon them while they remain on the right path."
(Saheeh al-Bukhaaree).

Notes

'Oh Allaah, I ask You to grant me Paradise and I take refuge in You from the Fire.' (Collected in Saheeh Ibn Maajah 1 328)

Notes

Rabee'a ath-Thaanee

28th

Kathir Ibn 'Ubayd said, "I visited 'Aishah, the Umm al-Mu'mineen, may Allaah be pleased with her. She said, 'Wait until I sew up my garment.' So I waited and said, 'Umm al-Mu'mineen, when I go out, I will inform them that your opponent is someone's miserliness.' She said, 'Concern yourself with your own business. There are no new clothes for anyone who does not wear well-worn clothes.'"
(Authenticated by Sheikh Al-Albaanee in Saheeh 'Adab al-Mufrad: 367)

Notes

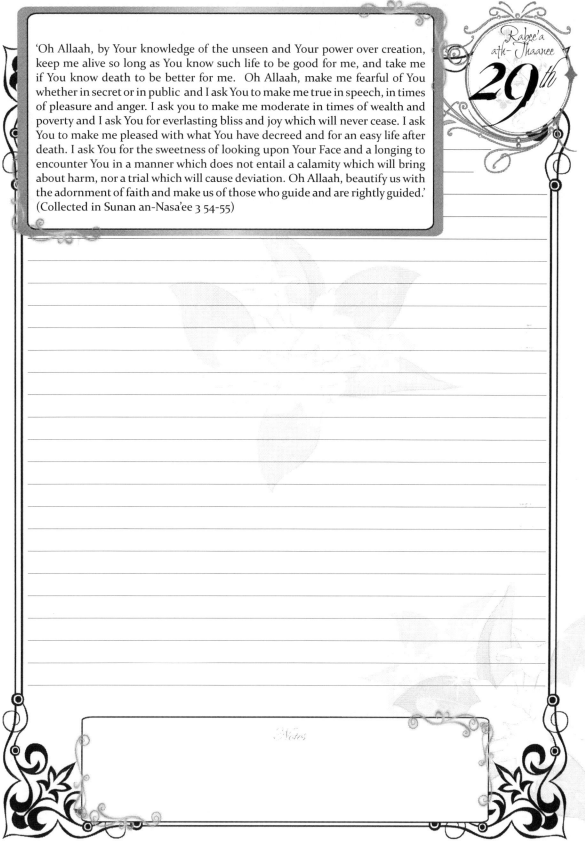

Rabee'a
ath-Thaanee
29th

'Oh Allaah, by Your knowledge of the unseen and Your power over creation, keep me alive so long as You know such life to be good for me, and take me if You know death to be better for me. Oh Allaah, make me fearful of You whether in secret or in public and I ask You to make me true in speech, in times of pleasure and anger. I ask you to make me moderate in times of wealth and poverty and I ask You for everlasting bliss and joy which will never cease. I ask You to make me pleased with what You have decreed and for an easy life after death. I ask You for the sweetness of looking upon Your Face and a longing to encounter You in a manner which does not entail a calamity which will bring about harm, nor a trial which will cause deviation. Oh Allaah, beautify us with the adornment of faith and make us of those who guide and are rightly guided.' (Collected in Sunan an-Nasa'ee 3 54-55)

Notes

'Musa Ibn Ismaa'eel said, "If I were to say to all of you that I never saw Hamaad Ibn Salamah laughing, I would have spoken truthfully. He was always busy either in narrating or reading, or remembering Allaah, or in ritual prayer. Indeed he divided up his days upon such matters."
(Siyaar 'Alaam an-Nubala: vol. 7, page 448)

Notes

Rabee'a
ath-Thaanee

...an extra journal page

Notes

Jumada al-Awwal

1438
JAN /FEB 2017

Yawm al-Sabt Saturday	*Yawm al-Ahad* Sunday	*Yawm al-Ithnayn* Monday	*Yawm ath-Thulatha* Tuesday	*Yawm al-Arbi'a* Wednesday	*Yawm al-Khamees* Thursday	*Yawm al-Jumu'ah* Friday
	1 29	2 30	3 31	4 1	5 2	6 3
7 4	8 5	9 6	10 7	11 8	12 9	13 10
14 11	15 12	16 13	17 14	18 15	19 16	20 17
21 18	22 19	23 20	24 21	25 22	26 23	27 24
28 25	29 26	30 27				

"-The best profit of this world is gained by always occupying yourself with that which is of most value and most beneficial for you in the next world. So how could someone intelligent sell away the rewards of Paradise for what he receives through some passing temporary desire?!

-If it was possible that knowledge could truly be considered beneficial without it being acted upon, then Allaah the Most Perfect would not have blamed and censured those clergy and priests from among the People of the Book who had previously received scriptures. And if deeds could be considered beneficial without their being based upon a sincere intention to do it for Allaah alone, then certainly Allaah would not have censured the hypocrites who lack this."

(Sheikh al-Islaam Ibn Qayyim in his work "*al-Fawaid*", page 31

"'Aishah reported that the Prophet, may Allaah's praise and salutations be upon him, said, "Forgive the people of good character and ways their slips." (Authenticated by Sheikh Al-Albaanee in Saheeh 'Adab al-Mufrad: 362)

Notes

Narrated Abu Hurairah: The Prophet said, "Allaah will give shade to seven types of people under His Shade on the Day of Resurrection. One of them will be a person who remembers Allaah and his eyes are then flooded with tears." (Saheeh al-Bukhaaree)

Notes

Abu ad-Darda' reported that the Prophet, may Allaah's praise and salutations be upon him, said, "Whoever has been given his portion of compassion has been given his portion of good. Whoever is denied being given his portion of compassion has been denied his portion of good. Good character will be the weightiest thing in the believer's balance on the Day of Rising. Allaah hates a crude, foul-mouthed person."

(Authenticated by Sheikh Al-Albaanee in Saheeh 'Adab al-Mufrad: 361)

Notes

Jumada al-Awwal
4th

"Has not the time come for the hearts of those who believe in the worship of Allaah alone to be affected by Allaah's Reminder, and that which has been revealed of the truth, lest they become as those who received the Scripture before, Jews and Christians, and the term was prolonged for them and so their hearts were hardened? And many of them were rebellious and disobedient to Allaah". (Surah al-Hadeed: 16)

Notes

Narrated Abu Musa: Allaah's Messenger, may Allaah's praise and salutations be upon him, said, "My example and the example of the message with which Allaah has sent me is like that of a man who came to some people and said, "I have seen with my own eyes the enemy forces, and I am a clear warner to you. So save yourself, save yourself! A group of them obeyed him and went out at night, slowly and stealthily and were safe, while another group did not believe him and thus the army took them in the morning and destroyed them." (Saheeh al-Bukhaaree)

Notes

The Prophet, may Allaah's praise and salutations be upon him, said, "Allaah Almighty revealed to me that you should be humble and that you should not commit wrongs against each other."
(Authenticated by Sheikh Al-Albaanee in Saheeh 'Adab al-Mufrad: 329)

Notes

Matraf Ibn 'Abdullah al-'Amree said, "Even if I were able to take out my heart and place it in my right hand, I would not be able to put anything into my heart, until Allaah placed it there." (Siyaar 'Alaam an-Nubala: Vol 4, page 190)

Jumada al-Awwal 7th

Notes

"He it is Who has sent His Messenger with guidance and the religion of truth -Islaam, that He may make it superior to all religions. And All-Sufficient is Allaah as a Witness. Oh wives of the Prophet! You are not like any other women. If you keep your duty to Allaah, then be not soft in speech, lest he in whose heart is a disease should be moved with desire, but speak in an honorable manner. And stay in your houses, and do not display yourselves like that of the times of ignorance, and perform the ritual prayers, and give the obligatory charity, and obey Allaah and His Messenger. Allaah wishes only to remove evil deeds and sins from you, Oh members of the family of the Prophet, and to purify you with a thorough purification."
(Surah al-Fath:28-33)

Notes

Abu Hurairah said that the Messenger of Allaah, may Allaah's praise and salutations be upon him, said, "Do you wish to strive in the making of supplication? Then you should say, 'Allaah assist me in being grateful to you, remembering you, and worshiping you well.' "
(Authentic by Sheikh al-Albaanee in Silsilaat As-Saheehah: 844 & Sheikh Muqbil in al-Saheeh al-Musnad: 1355)

Notes

Abee Hazm al-Madanee said, "Look towards that which will rectify yourself and act upon it, even if it is something considered evil by the general people, and look towards that which will bring evil to you and repel it from you, even if it is something considered beneficial by the general people."
(Siyaar 'Alaam an-Nubala: vol. 6, page 98)

Notes

Abu ad-Darda' reported that the Prophet, may Allaah's praise and salutations be upon him, said, "Shall I tell you a degree better than prayer, fasting and charity?" "Yes," they replied. He went to say, "Improving the state of relations with your associates. Whereas causing strife and problems in the state of relations with your associates is what shaves away and harms."
(Authenticated by Sheikh Al-Albaanee in Saheeh 'Adab al-Mufrad: 303)

Notes

"Then when their Messengers came to them with clear proofs, they were pleased and proud with that which they had of the knowledge of worldly things. And that at which they used to mock, surrounded them (the punishment). So when they saw Our punishment, they said, 'We believe in Allaah Alone and reject all that we used to associate with Him as His partners.' Then their faith could not help them when already they saw Our punishment. Like this has been the way of Allaah in dealing with His slaves. And there the disbelievers lost utterly when Our torment covered them." (Surah Ghaafir:83-85)

Notes

Abu Umama related that the Messenger of Allaah, may Allaah's praise and salutations be upon him, said, "Anyone who shows mercy, even to an animal meant for slaughtering, will be shown mercy by Allaah on the Day of Rising." (Authenticated by Sheikh Al-Albaanee in Saheeh 'Adab al-Mufrad: 294)

Jumada al-Awwal

13th

Notes

Jumada al-Awwal 14th

Narrated Anas: The Prophet, may Allaah's praise and salutations be upon him, said, "If you knew that which I know, you would laugh little and weep much." (Saheeh al-Bukhaaree)

Notes

"So be patient; verily, the Promise of Allaah is true and whether We show you some part of what We have promised them, or We cause you to die, then still it is to Us they all shall be returned. And, indeed We have sent Messengers before you; of some of them We have related to you their story. And of some We have not related to you their story, and it was not given to any Messenger that he should bring a sign except by the Leave of Allaah. But, when comes the Commandment of Allaah, the matter will be decided with truth, and the followers of falsehood will then lose everything." (Surah Ghaafir:77-78)

Notes

The doing of good was mentioned when some people were sitting with Imaam Ahmad. And it was said that it is considered less than gaining knowledge. So he replied to them, "Be quiet! Does one intend through gaining knowledge anything else than what it enables of the doing of good?!"
(Siyaar 'Alaam an-Nubala: vol. 9, page 340)

Notes

Abu Dharr said, "I asked, 'Messenger of Allaah, what if a man loves a people but cannot join them?' He replied, 'Abu Dharr, you are with the one you love.' I said, 'I love Allaah and His Messenger.' He said, 'Abu Dharr, you are with the one you love.'"

(Authenticated by Sheikh Al-Albaanee in Saheeh 'Adab al-Mufrad: 269)

Notes

Jumada al-Awwal 18th

"And whoever does evil or wrongs himself but afterwards seeks Allaah's forgiveness, he will find Allaah Oft-Forgiving, Most Merciful. And whoever earns sin, he earns it only against himself. And Allaah is Ever All-Knowing, All-Wise. And whoever earns a fault or a sin and then throws it onto someone innocent, he has indeed burdened himself with falsehood and a manifest sin." (Surah an-Nisaa:110-112)

Notes

Narrated 'Abdullah Ibn 'Amr: The Prophet, may Allaah's praise and salutations be upon him, said, "A Muslim is the one who avoids harming Muslims with his tongue or his hands. And a muhaajir, or emigrant, is the one who gives up all which Allaah has forbidden."
(Saheeh al-Bukhaaree)

Notes

"When two parties from among you were about to lose heart, except that Allaah was their Supporter and Protector. And in Allaah should the believers put their trust. And Allaah has already made you victorious at Badr, when you were a weak little force. So fear Allaah much that you may be grateful. Remember when you (Oh Muhammad) said to the believers, 'Is it not enough for you that your Lord should help you with three thousand angels sent down?' Indeed, if you hold onto patience and piety, and the enemy comes rushing towards you; your Lord will help you with five thousand angels having marks of distinction. Allaah made it not but as a message of good news for you and as an assurance to your hearts. And there is no victory except from Allaah, the All-Mighty, the All-Wise."
(Surah Aal-'Imraan:123-126)

Notes

Hukaym Ibn Sa'd heard 'Ali say, "Do not be hasty, spreading and divulging secrets. As ahead of you lies severe, difficult afflictions, long lasting strife, and oppressive and heavy trials."
(Authenticated by Sheikh Al-Albaanee in Saheeh 'Adab al-Mufrad: 250)

Notes

Narrated Abu Hurairah: Allaah's Messenger, may Allaah's praise and salutations be upon him, said, "If any one of you looked at a person who was made superior to him in property and in good appearance, then he should also look at the one who is inferior to him, and to whom he has been made superior." (Saheeh al-Bukhaaree)

Notes

Sulaymaan Ibn 'Abdul-Maalik made Hajj with 'Umar Ibn 'Abdul-'Azeez, and then one night they encountered a rain storm with such lighting and peals of thunder that their hearts almost were torn apart during it. Afterward Sulayman said, "Oh Abu Hafs, have you ever seen night like that? Or heard anything like that before?" 'Umar Ibn 'Abdul-'Azeez replied, "Oh Leader of the faithful, this was the voice of Allaah's mercy, how would it have been if we had heard the voice of His wrath and punishment?"
(Siyaar 'Alaam an-Nubala: vol. 5, page 121)

Notes

Ali Ibn Abi Taalib said, "The person who says something indecent and the person who makes it known are equal as far as the wrongdoing is concerned." (Authenticated by Sheikh Al-Albaanee in Saheeh 'Adab al-Mufrad: 246)

Notes

"And Allaah has preferred some of you to others in wealth and properties. Then, those who are preferred will by no means hand over their wealth and properties to those slaves whom their right hands possess, so that they may be equal with them in respect thereof. Do they then deny the Favour of Allaah? And Allaah has made for you mates or wives of your own kind, and has made for you, from your wives, sons and grandsons, and has bestowed on you good provision. Do they then believe in false deities and deny the favor of Allaah by not worshipping Allaah Alone? And they worship others besides Allaah such as do not and cannot own any provision for them from the heavens or the earth." (Surah an-Nahl:71-73)

Jumada al-Awwal 25th

Notes

Narrated 'Abdullah Ibn 'Umar: I heard Allaah's Messenger, may Allaah's praise and salutations be upon him, saying, "People are just like camels, out of one hundred, one can hardly find a single camel suitable to ride." (Saheeh al-Bukhaaree)

Notes

"Indeed in the Messenger of Allaah you have a good example to follow for him who hopes for the Meeting with Allaah and the Last Day, and remembers Allaah often." (Surah al-Ahzaab:021)

Jumada al-Awwal 27th

Notes

Asma' bint Yazid reported that the Prophet, may Allaah's praise and salutations be upon him, said, "Shall I tell you who is the best of you?" "Yes," they replied. He said, "Those who remind you of Allaah when you see them." He went on to say, "Shall I tell you who is the worst from amongst you?" "Yes," they replied. He said, "Those who go about slandering, causing mischief between friends in order to separate them, and desiring to lead the innocent into wrongdoing." (Authenticated by Sheikh Al-Albaanee in Saheeh 'Adab al-Mufrad: 246)

Notes

'Aishah narrated that the Messenger of Allaah, may Allaah's praise and salutations be upon him, would supplicate, "Oh Allaah as you have made my appearance good, also make my character good."
(Authenticated by Sheikh al-Albaanee in Saheeh al-Jaam'ea: 1307 & Sheikh Muqbil in al-Jaame'a as-Saheeh, vol. 2 page 448)

Notes

Narrated Mu'adh Ibn Jabal: While I was riding behind the Prophet as a companion rider and there was nothing between me and him except the back of the saddle, he said, "Oh Mu'adh!" I replied, "Labbaik Oh Allaah's Messenger! And Sa'diak!" He proceeded for a while and then said, "Oh Mu'adh!" I said, "Labbaik and Sa'daik, Oh Allaah's Messenger!" He then proceeded for another while and said, "Oh Mu'adh Ibn Jabal!" I replied, "Labbaik, Oh Allaah's Messenger, and Sa'daik!" He said, "Do you know what Allaah's right on His slaves is?" I replied, "Allaah and His Messenger know better." He said, "Allaah's right on His worshipers is that they should worship Him and not worship anything besides Him." He then proceeded for a while, and again said, "Oh Mu'adh Ibn Jabal!" I replied. "Labbaik, Oh Allaah's Messenger, and Sa'daik." He said, "Do you know what the right of Allaah's worshipers' on Allaah is if they did that?" I replied, "Allaah and His Messenger know better." He said, "The right of Allaah's slaves on Allaah is that He should not punish them if they did that." The example of the believer with regard to imaan is like the example of a horse with regards to its tethering stake; it roams around and then returns to its tethering stake, and the believer is negligent and then he turns back to his imaan. So feed the pious with your food and treat the believers well. (Saheeh al-Bukhaaree)

Notes

...an extra journal page

Notes

Jumada ath-Thaanee

1438
FEB / MAR 2017

Youm al-Sabt Saturday	Youm al-Ahad Sunday	Youm al-Ithnayn Monday	Youm ath-Thilatha Tuesday	Youm al-Arbo'a Wednesday	Youm al-Khamees Thursday	Youm al-Jumi'ah Friday
			1 28	2 1	3 2	4 3
5 4	6 5	7 6	8 7	9 8	10 9	11 10
12 11	13 12	14 13	15 14	16 15	17 16	18 17
19 18	20 19	21 20	22 21	23 22	24 23	25 24
26 25	27 26	28 27	29 28			

"*If the worshiper of Allaah encounters those decreed matters that he dislikes, his perspective towards them should encompass six aspects:*
The first aspect is affirming the right of Allaah to be worshiped alone, and that Allaah is the One who decreed this matter to occur, willed this, and brought it forth, always remembering that whatever Allaah wishes will be and whatever He does not wish does not occur.
The second aspect is affirming its fairness- that within it there is found His way of justice and His perfect judgment
The third aspect is the affirming of His overriding mercy within everything which He has decreed and which has predominance over His anger and His retribution, as certainly His mercy is prevailing and preponderant." (continued...)

(Sheikh al-Islaam Ibn Qayyim in his work "*al-Fawaid*", page 32)

Abee Hazm al-Madanee said, "Anything you do not want to be with you in the Hereafter, leave it today." And he said, "Consider every deed due to which you hate to meet death and so turn away from it, then it will not harm you when you die."   (Siyaar 'Alaam an-Nubala: vol. 6, page 98)

Jumada al-Thaanee 1st

Notes

'Abdullah said, "The most blameworthy thing in a believer's character is crudeness."
(Authenticated by Sheikh Al-Albaanee in Saheeh 'Adab al-Mufrad:239)

Notes

"Verily, the Muslims, those who submit to Allaah in Islaam, men and women, the believers, men and women, the men and the women who are obedient to Allaah, the men and women who are truthful in their speech and deeds, the men and the women who are patient in performing all the duties which Allaah has ordered and in abstaining from all that Allaah has forbidden, the men and the women who are humble before their Lord, Allaah, the men and the women who give charity, the men and the women who observe the obligatory and optional fasting, the men and the women who guard their chastity from illegal sexual acts and the men and the women who remember Allaah much with their hearts and tongues- Allaah has prepared for them forgiveness and a great reward." (Surah al-Ahzaab:035)

Notes

Jumada al-Thaanee 4th

Anas reported that the Messenger of Allaah, may Allaah's praise and salutations be upon him, said, "Oh Allaah, there is nothing that is easy except that which you make easy, and if you wish, then you make the difficult matter easy." (Authentic by Sheikh al-Albaanee in Silsilaat As-Saheehah: 2886 & Sheikh Muqbil in al-Saheeh al-Musnad: 71)

Notes

Narrated Ghailan: Anas said, "You people do bad deeds -commit sins- which seem in your eyes as tiny and smaller than a hair, while we used to consider those very deeds during the lifetime of the Prophet as destructive sins." (Saheeh al-Bukhaaree)

Notes

Jumada al-Thaanee

6th

"Allaah does not like that the evil should be uttered in public except by him who has been wronged. And Allaah is Ever All-Hearer, All-Knower. Whether you (mankind) disclose by good words of thanks a good deed done to you in the form of a favor by someone, or conceal it, or pardon an evil. Verily, Allaah is Ever Oft-Pardoning, All-Powerful. (Surah an-Nisaa:148-149)

Notes

'Aishah reported that some Jews came to the Prophet, may Allaah's praise and salutations be upon him, and said, "Poison ('using the Arabic word sam' instead of 'salam') be upon you." 'Aishah said, "And upon you, and may the curse of Allaah and the anger of Allaah be upon you!" The Prophet said, "Easy, 'Aishah, you must be gentle. Beware of harshness and coarseness." She asked, "Didn't you hear what they said?" He said, "Didn't you hear what I said? I repeated it to them yet what I said about them will be accepted and what they said about me will not be accepted."
(Authenticated by Sheikh Al-Albaanee in Saheeh 'Adab al-Mufrad: 236)

Notes

Narrated Jundub: The Prophet, may Allaah's praise and salutations be upon him, said, "He who lets the people hear of his good deeds intentionally, to win their praise, Allaah will let the people know his real intention on the Day of Resurrection. And he who does good things in public to show off and win the praise of the people, Allaah will disclose his real intention and thus humiliate him." (Saheeh al-Bukhaaree)

Notes

"And those who annoy believing men and women undeservedly, they bear on themselves the crime of slander and plain sin. Oh Prophet! Tell your wives and your daughters and the women of the believers to draw their cloaks all over their bodies. That will be better that they should be known as free, respectable women so as not to be annoyed. And Allaah is Ever Oft-Forgiving, Most Merciful." (Surah al-Ahzaab:059)

Notes

Jabir reported that the Messenger of Allaah, may Allaah's praise and salutations be upon him, said, "Every act of kindness is charity. Part of kindness is that you offer your brother a cheerful face and you pour some of the water in your bucket into his."
(Authenticated by Sheikh Al-Albaanee in Saheeh 'Adab al-Mufrad:)

Notes

Narrated 'Ubada Ibn As-Samit: The Prophet said, "Whoever loves to meet Allaah, Allaah (too) loves to meet him. And who-ever hates to meet Allaah, Allaah (too) hates to meet him". 'Aishah, or some of the wives of the Prophet, said, "But we dislike death." He said, "This is not what is intended. Rather, it is meant that when the time of the death of a believer approaches, he receives the good news of Allaah's pleasure with him and His blessings upon him, and so at that time nothing is dearer to him than what is in front of him. He therefore loves the meeting with Allaah, and Allaah too loves the meeting with him. But when the time of the death of a disbeliever approaches, he receives the evil news of Allaah's torment and His Requital, whereupon nothing is more hateful to him than what is before him. Therefore, he hates the meeting with Allaah, and Allaah too, hates the meeting with him." (Saheeh al-Bukhaaree)

Notes

Jumada
al-Thaanee
12th

"Oh Allaah, I ask You for knowledge which is beneficial and sustenance which is good, and deeds which are acceptable." (Supplication after giving salaam for the fajr prayer: Collected in Saheeh Ibn Maajah 1 152)

Notes

"Some of the rulers asked 'Umar Ibn Dhar about the issue of Qadr, or Allaah's decree. So he replied, "There is a matter here which will preoccupy us from this issue of Qadr." They asked, "What is it?" He said, "That final night which the next coming morning will be the beginning of the Day of Judgment." Then he cried at this, and they cried with him."
(Siyaar 'Alaam an-Nubala: vol. 6, page 387)

Notes

Mu'adh Ibn 'Abdullah Ibn Khubayb al-Juhani related from his father that his uncle said that the Messenger of Allaah, may Allaah's praise and salutations be upon him, came out to them with the traces of ghusl on himself. "He had a cheerful manner. We thought that he was with his wives. We said, 'Messenger of Allaah, we see that you are cheerful.' He said, 'Yes, and praise be to Allaah!' Then wealth was mentioned, so that the Messenger of Allaah, may Allaah's praise and salutations be upon him, said, 'There is no harm in wealth for someone who has the fear of Allaah, but health for the person who has fear of Allaah is even better than wealth. And cheerfulness is a blessing.'" (Authenticated by Sheikh Al-Albaanee in Saheeh 'Adab al-Mufrad: 231)

Notes

Anas Ibn Maalik said, "A man passed by the Prophet, may Allaah's praise and salutations be upon him, while he was with some other people. One of the men who was with him said, 'Indeed I love this man for Allaah.' The Prophet, may Allaah's praise and salutations be upon him, asked him, 'Have you informed him of this?' He replied, 'No.' So the Prophet, may Allaah's praise and salutations be upon him, said, 'Go to him and inform him.' So the man went and informed the man who had passed, who replied, 'I love you for the sake of the One who you love me for.' The man returned back to the Prophet, may Allaah's praise and salutations be upon him, who said to him, 'You are with the one you love, and you are given the rewards of what you did.' (Authenticated by Sheikh al-Albaanee in Silsilaat As-Saheehah: under 418 & Sheikh Muqbil in as-Saheeh al-Musnad: 52)

Jumada al-Thaanee
15th

Notes

Narrated Abu Qatada Ibn Rabee'a Al-Ansari: A funeral procession passed by Allaah's Messenger, who said, "Relieved or relieving?" The people asked, "Oh Allaah's Messenger! What is relieved and relieving?" He said, "A believer is relieved by death from the troubles and hardships of the world and leaves for the Mercy of Allaah, while the death of a wicked person relieves the people, the land, the trees, and the animals from him." (Saheeh al-Bukhaaree)

Notes

Mihsan al-Ansari reported that the Prophet, may Allaah's praise and salutations be upon him, said, "When someone is secure in his property, healthy in his body and has his food for the day, it is as if he owned the entire world." (Authenticated by Sheikh Al-Albaanee in Saheeh 'Adab al-Mufrad: 230)

Notes

Narrated Ibn 'Umar: Allaah's Messenger, may Allaah's praise and salutations be upon him, said, "When any one of you dies, his destination is displayed before him in the morning and in the afternoon, either in the Hellfire or in Paradise, and it is said to him, 'That is your place till you are resurrected and sent to it.' (Saheeh al-Bukhaaree)

Notes

Fudhail Ibn 'Ayadh said, "Indeed yesterday is a lesson for us, today is for doing good deeds, and tomorrow is what we have hope for."
(Siyaar 'Alaam an-Nubala: vol. 8, page 427)

Notes

It is reported Nawwas Ibn Sam'an asked the Messenger of Allaah, may Allaah's praise and salutations be upon him, about dutifulness and wrong action. He said, "Goodness is good character and wrongdoing is that which bothers and irritates you within yourself and which you dislike for other people to become aware of."
(Authenticated by Sheikh Al-Albaanee in Saheeh 'Adab al-Mufrad: 226)

Notes

Warrad, the scribe of al-Mughira Ibn Shu'ba, said, "Mu'awiya wrote to al-Mughira Ibn Shu'ba, saying, 'Write down for me something which you heard from the Messenger of Allaah, may Allaah's praise and salutations be upon him.' Al-Mughira wrote to him, ' The Messenger of Allaah, may Allaah's praise and salutations be upon him, used to forbid gossip, wasting money, asking too many questions, refusing to give, disobedience to parents and burying daughters alive."
(Authenticated by Sheikh Al-Albaanee in Saheeh 'Adab al-Mufrad: 228)

Notes

"Oh you who believe! Save yourselves and your families Hellfire whose fuel is men and stones!" (Surah at- Tahreem: 6)

Notes

"Each of you is a guardian and is responsible for those whom he is in charge of. So the ruler is a guardian and is responsible for his subjects; a man is the guardian of his family and is responsible for those under his care; a woman is a guardian of her husband's home and is responsible for those under her care; a servant is the guardian of his master's wealth and is responsible for that which he is entrusted with; and a man is the guardian of his father's wealth and is responsible for what is under his care. So each one of you is a guardian and is responsible for what he is entrusted with."
(Saheeh al-Bukhaaree: 252 and Saheeh Muslim: 4496)

Notes

Fath al-Mausoolee said, "The one whose practice is to continually examine his heart- through this he is bestowed with happiness and joy in Allaah."
(Siyaar 'Alaam an-Nubala: vol. 10, page 484)

Notes

'Abdullah Ibn 'Amr said, "There are four qualities such that if you were to be given them, you will not be harmed even if the world were to be taken away from you. They are: good character, restraint in eating your food, truthful words, and upholding a trust."
(Authenticated by Sheikh Al-Albaanee in Saheeh 'Adab al-Mufrad: 221)

Notes

Jumada al-Thaanee

26th

It is narrated on the authority of 'Usamah Ibn Shareek that some people said to the Messenger of Allaah, may Allaah's praise and salutations be upon him, "Oh Messenger of Allaah, what is the best thing that can be given to a Muslim?" He replied, "Good character."
(Authenticated by Sheikh al-Albaanee in Saheeh Ibn Maajah: 2789 & Sheikh Muqbil in al-Saheeh al-Musnad: 17)

Notes

"And your Lord has decreed that you worship none but Him. And that you be dutiful to your parents. If one of them or both of them attain old age in your life, say not to them a word of disrespect, nor shout at them, but address them in terms of honor." (Surah al-Israa':023)

Notes

Narrated Anas: The Prophet had a she-camel called Al'Adba' and it was too fast to be beaten in races. There came a Bedouin riding a camel of his, and that camel outran Al-Adba'. That result was hard on the Muslims, who said sorrowfully, "Al- Adba has been outrun." Allaah's Messenger, may Allaah's praise and salutations be upon him, said, "It is due from Allaah that nothing would be raised high in this world except that He lowers or puts it down." (Saheeh al-Bukhaaree)

Notes

Abu Hurairah said, "I heard Abu al-Qaasim say, 'The best of you in Islam is the best of you in character when they possess understanding of the religion." (Authenticated by Sheikh Al-Albaanee in Saheeh 'Adab al-Mufrad: 218)

Jumada
al-Thaanee
29th

Notes

Saaleh Ibn Ahmad Ibn Hanbal said, "I used to often hear my father recite Surat al-Kahf and he would often say, 'Oh Allaah rescue me, rescue me.'"

Hamad Ibn Zayd said, "Yahya Ibn Sa'eed al-Ansaaree would often say in his sittings, 'Oh Allaah rescue me, rescue me.'" (Siyaar 'Alaam an-Nubala: vol. 11, page 222 & : vol. 4, page 222)

Notes

...an extra journal page

Notes

Rajab

1438

MAR / APR 2017

Yaum al-Sabt Saturday	*Yaum al-Ahad* Sunday	*Yaum al-Ithnayn* Monday	*Yaum ath-Thulatha* Tuesday	*Yaum al-Arbi'a* Wednesday	*Yaum al-Khamees* Thursday	*Yaum al-Jumi'ah* Friday
				1 29	**2** 30	**3** 31
4 1	**5** 2	**6** 3	**7** 4	**8** 5	**9** 6	**10** 7
11 8	**12** 9	**13** 10	**14** 11	**15** 12	**16** 13	**17** 14
18 15	**19** 16	**20** 17	**21** 18	**22** 19	**23** 20	**24** 21
25 22	**26** 23	**27** 24	**28** 25	**29** 26		

"If the worshiper of Allaah encounters those decreed matters that he dislikes, his perspective towards it should encompass six aspects: (...continued)

Fourthly, the aspect of the proper way of viewing it, and affirming its wisdom- that the wisdom of Allaah the Most Perfect, must require that specific matter, that He did not decree it without a purpose nor simply for play. Fifthly, is in regard to praise, as indeed complete praise is due to Allaah, the Most Perfect, from every direction. The Sixth is in relation to the truth of you being one whose state is that of full compliance to Allaah's will; that you only stand as a complete slave of Allaah, proceeding under every kind of judgment coming from your Master, Who rules over you due to you being His property and His slave. So Allaah has placed you under His general decrees just as He has also placed you under the obligation to adhere to His desired religious directives."

(Sheikh al-Islaam Ibn Qayyim in his work *"al-Fawaid"*, page 43)

Shaykh al-Islaam Ibn Taymiyyah said, "There is no doubt that the remembrances and supplications are from the best forms of worship. Worship is built upon adherence to what the source texts state and following them...therefore it is not allowed for anyone to legislate new forms of remembrance and supplications and take them as actions of worship that the people must constantly perform just as they constantly perform the five daily prayers. Rather this is innovating into the religion that which Allaah has not given permission for. However, if a person were to supplicate with these new supplication on occasion and individually without making this supplication a Sunnah for the people, then this would not be an innovation. As for the one who takes to a devised formula of remembrance that has not been legislated and makes this to be a Sunnah to be followed then this is from those things which are forbidden. Additionally, the legislated supplications and remembrance contain all the correct goals and all the lofty intentions that a person could ever require and no one but an ignorant one or an extremist would turn away from these and recourse to these newly invented remembrance. (Majmou' Fataawaa: 22 510)

Notes

Abu Musaa narrated, "We were in the company of the Messenger of Allaah, may Allaah's praise and salutations be upon him. Whenever we went up a high place we used to say the takbeer –Allaahu akbar- and tahleel –La ilaha illAllaah- loudly. The Prophet, may Allaah's praise and salutations be upon him, said, 'Oh People be merciful to yourselves for you are not calling upon one who is deaf or absent. Indeed He is with you, indeed He Sees and is close." Imaam Ibn Hajr al-Asqalaanee said in Fath al-Baaree:6 166, "at-Tabaree said, 'This hadeeth constitutes evidence that is disliked to raise one's voice when supplicating and performing remembrance, this was the opinion generally of the first generation from the Companions and from that generation which came after them.' (Saheeh al-Bukhaaree)

Notes

The Messenger of Allaah, may Allaah's praise and salutations be upon him, said, "Indeed amazing are the affairs of a believer! They are all for his benefit; If he is granted ease of living he is thankful; and this is best for him. And if he is afflicted with a hardship, he perseveres; and this is best for him." (Saheeh Muslim)

Rajab
3rd

Notes

"Certainly, We shall test you with fear, hunger, loss of wealth, lives and fruits; but give glad tidings to the patient - those who, when afflicted with calamity say, 'Truly to Allaah we belong, and truly to Him shall we return.' it is those who will be awarded blessings and mercy from their Lord; and it is those who are the guided ones." (Surah al-Baqarah:155-157)

Notes

Abu Hurairah and Ka'b Bin Maalik reported that the Prophet, may Allaah's praise and salutations be upon him, said,
"The parable of a believer is that of a fresh and moist plant; the wind tilts it this way and that way; and so is the believer; he continues to be subject to affliction. And the parable of a hypocrite is that of a firm cedar tree; it does not wave until it is uprooted and overturned all at once."
(Saheeh al-Bukhaaree and Saheeh Muslim)

Notes

Al-Maymoonee said, "I asked Aboo 'Abdullaah Imaam Ahmad, 'Which is more beloved to you, that I should I begin teaching my son the Qur'aan or the hadeeth?' He said, 'No! The Qur'aan.' I said, 'Shall I teach him all of it?' He replied, 'Unless that is difficult, in which case teach him some of it.' Then he said to me, 'If he begins reciting first, then he will learn correct recitation and will persevere in it.' (Related by Ibn Muflih in al-Aadaabush-Shar'eeyyah.)

Notes

As for seeking to memorize the Qur'an then this is to be given preference over many of the things that the people consider to be knowledge, but are – in reality – either totally useless, or having little benefit. It is also to be given precedence in learning, especially by those who wish to acquire knowledge of the religion, its principles and its particulars. Since what is prescribed for such a person at this time is that he should begin by memorizing the Qur'an, as it is the foundation of the branches of knowledge of the Religion. This is contrary to what is done by many of the people of innovation, in that one of them will preoccupy himself with superfluous parts of knowledge; such as theological rhetoric and argumentation; or very rare matters of differences; and blind following, which there is no need for; or very strange and rare hadeeth narrations which are not established, nor of benefit; and many discussions do not establish proofs. And he abandons memorizing the Qur'aan which is more important than all of this."
(Sheikh al-Islaam Ibn Taymeeyah Fataawa al-Kubraa: 2 54-55).

Notes

Rajab

8th

Anas reported that the Prophet, may Allaah's praise and salutations be upon him, passed by some people who were wrestling. He asked, "What is this?" They said, "So-and-so is the strongest, he can beat anybody." The Prophet, may Allaah's praise and salutations be upon him, said, "Shall I not tell you who is even stronger than him? The man who, when he is mistreated by another, controls his anger, has defeated his own shaytaan and the shaytaan of the one who made him angry."
(Reported by al-Bazzaar, Authenticated Ibn Hajr in Fath al-Baree, 10 519)

Notes

"There are no days during which good deeds are more beloved by Allaah than these (ten) days." Prophet, may Allaah's praise and salutations be upon him, was then asked, "Not even jihaad in Allaah's way?" He replied, "Not even jihaad in Allaah's way; except for a person who went out (for jihaad) with his self and wealth and came back with none (i.e. lost all for Allaah)."
(Authenticated by Sheikh al-Albaanee in Irwaa' ul-Ghaleel: 953)

Notes

Muhammad Ibnul-Fadl said, "I heard my grandfather say, 'I asked my father for permission to study under Qutaybah, so he said, "First learn the Qur'aan and then I will give you permission." So I memorized the Qur'aan by heart. Then he said to me, "Remain until you have led the people in prayer with the taraaweeh prayer." So I did so, and after the 'Eed Prayer he gave me permission, so I left for Marw."
(Related by adh-Dhahabee in Tadhkiratul-Huffaadh: 2 722)

Notes

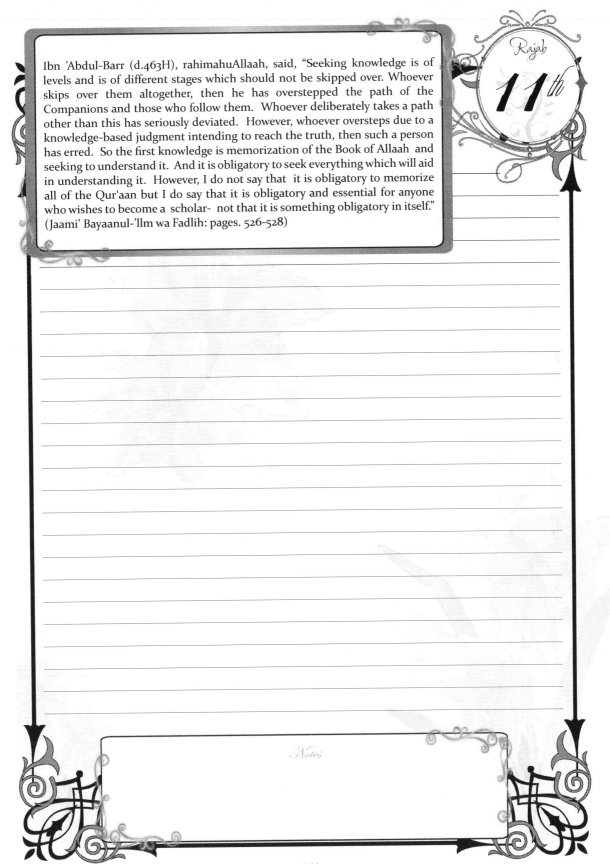

Ibn 'Abdul-Barr (d.463H), rahimahuAllaah, said, "Seeking knowledge is of levels and is of different stages which should not be skipped over. Whoever skips over them altogether, then he has overstepped the path of the Companions and those who follow them. Whoever deliberately takes a path other than this has seriously deviated. However, whoever oversteps due to a knowledge-based judgment intending to reach the truth, then such a person has erred. So the first knowledge is memorization of the Book of Allaah and seeking to understand it. And it is obligatory to seek everything which will aid in understanding it. However, I do not say that it is obligatory to memorize all of the Qur'aan but I do say that it is obligatory and essential for anyone who wishes to become a scholar- not that it is something obligatory in itself."
(Jaami' Bayaanul-'llm wa Fadlih: pages. 526-528)

Notes

Rajab

12th

'Umar Ibn 'Abdul-Waahid, a companion of al-Awzaa'ee said, "We read in 'al-Muwattaa' to Imaam Maalik in forty days, so he said, 'A book that took me forty years to compile, yet you take from me in only forty days! How little you understand of it.' (Related by Ibn 'Abdul-Barr in at-Tamheed (1 77))

Notes

Al-Khateeb also said, "And know that the heart in an organ from the organs. It is able to bear some things and unable to bear others- just like the rest of the body. Thus, some people are able to carry one-hundred pounds, whereas others are unable to carry even twenty. Some people are able to walk a number of miles in a day without tiring, whereas others are unable to even walk a mile a day before they become tired...so let each person limit himself to what he is able without expending all his energies, because that will better aid him in learning with a good mind, from a firm and proficient teacher."
(Al-Faqeeh wal-Mutafaqqih: 2 107)

Rajab
13th

Notes

Rajab

14th

Umm Salamah said, "The Messenger of Allaah, may Allaah's praise and salutations be upon him, used to supplicate in the morning prayer, 'Oh Allaah! I ask you for beneficial knowledge, righteous action and pure sustenance.' (Authenticated by al-Haafidh Ibn Hajar in Nataa'ijul Afkaar- Al-Musnad of Imaam Ahmad: 6 305)

Notes

Anas Ibn Maalik narrated: I heard Messenger of Allaah, may Allaah's praise and salutations be upon him, supplicate, "Oh Allaah! Benefit me with knowledge. Teach me that which will benefit me, and provide me with knowledge from which I can derive benefit." (Authentically narrated in al-Mustradrak of Imam Haakim: 1 510 and he said: "It is authentic upon the condition of Muslim." Imaam Adh-Dhahabee agreed with this authentication.)

Notes

Rajab
16th

Sheikh-al-Islaam Ibn Taymiyyah said, "... with remembrance of Allaah and turning towards Him, Allaah guides such a person, as Allaah has said, "Oh My servants! All of you are misguided, except whomsoever I guide. So seek your guidance from me.' (Saheeh Muslim) And as the Prophet, may Allaah's praise and salutations be upon him, used to say, "Oh Allaah, Lord of Jibreel, Meekaa'eel and Israafeel. The Originator of the heavens and the earth. Knower of the Unseen and the apparent. You judge between Your servant in that which he differs. So guide me in that which I differ from the truth, by Your permission. Indeed, You guide whomsoever You please, to a Path which is straight." (Saheeh Muslim: 770) (Majmoo'ul Fataawaa: 4 39)

Notes

Narrated Abdullah Ibn Umar: The Prophet passed by a man who was admonishing his brother regarding Haya and was saying, "You are very shy, and I am afraid that might harm you." On that, Allaah's Messenger said, "Leave him, for modesty is a part of imaan." (Saheeh al-Bukhaaree)

Notes

Abu Hurairah reported that the Prophet, may Allaah's praise and salutations be upon him, climbed upon the mimbar and said, "Aameen aameen, aameen (meaning Oh Allaah grant it)." So it was said, "Oh Messenger of Allaah, why did you climb upon the mimbar and then say aameen, aameen, aameen"? So he said, "Jibreel came to me and said, 'Whoever reaches the month of Ramadan and does not have his sins forgiven and so enters Fire, then may Allaah distance him, say aameen.' So I said 'aameen'". (Authentically narrated in al-Musnad of Imaan Ahmad, Saheeh Ibn Khuzaymah, and others)

Notes

Abu Musa once related that the Prophet, may Allaah's praise and salutations be upon him, said, "The difference between the one who remembers his Lord and the one who does not is like the difference between the living and the dead." (Saheeh al-Bukhaaree: 11 208)

Notes

Rajab

20th

'Oh Allaah, distance me from my sins just as You have distanced the East from the West. Oh Allaah, purify me of my sins as a white robe is purified of filth, Oh Allaah, cleanse me of my sins with snow, water, and ice.' (Supplication at the start of the prayer after takbeer- Saheeh Al-Bukhaaree: 1 181 and Saheeh Muslim: 1 419)

Notes

"Allaah is Most Great, Allaah is Most Great, Allaah is Most Great, all praise is for Allaah, all praise is for Allaah, all praise is for Allaah, and I declare the perfection of Allaah in the early morning and in the late afternoon." (said three times) "I take refuge with Allaah from the devil, from his pride, his poetry and his madness."
(Collected in Saheeh Muslim 1 420, Sunan Abu Dawud 1 203, and others)

Rajab

21st

Notes

The Messenger of Allaah, may Allaah's praise and salutations be upon him, said, 'You shall not enter paradise until you believe, and you shall not believe until you love one another. Shall I not inform you of something, that if you were to act upon it, you will indeed achieve mutual love for one another? Spread the greeting amongst yourselves.' (Collected in Saheeh Muslim 2 891)

'Oh Allaah, to any believer whom I have insulted, let that be cause to draw him near to You on the Day of Resurrection.'
(Collected in Saheeh al-Bukhaaree 11 17 & Saheeh Muslim 2/891)

Notes

Sa'd said "We were sitting with the Messenger of Allaah, may Allaah's praise and salutations be upon him, and he said, 'Are any of you unable to gain a thousand good deeds each day?' Somebody then asked him, 'How does one achieve a thousand good deeds?' He replied, 'He should say, "Subhaanallaah (How perfect Allaah is) one hundred times, for a thousand good deeds are recorded for him or a thousand bad deeds are wiped away."'
(Collected in Saheeh Muslim 4 2073)

Rajab
23rd

Notes

Anas Ibn Maalik narrated: I heard Messenger of Allaah, may Allaah's praise and salutations be upon him, supplicate, "Oh Allaah! Benefit me with knowledge. Teach me that which will benefit me, and provide me with knowledge from which I can derive benefit." (Authentically narrated in al-Mustradrak of Imam Haakim: 1 510 and he said: "It is authentic upon the condition of Muslim." Imaam Adh-Dhahabee agreed with this authentication.)

Notes

Sheikh-al-Islaam Ibn Taymiyyah said,

"... with remembrance of Allaah and turning towards Him, Allaah guides such a person, as Allaah has said, "Oh My servants! All of you are misguided, except whomsoever I guide. So seek your guidance from me.' (Saheeh Muslim) And as the Prophet, may Allaah's praise and salutations be upon him, used to say, "Oh Allaah, Lord of Jibreel, Meekaa'eel and Israafeel, the Originator of the heavens and the earth, Knower of the Unseen and the apparent. You judge between Your servant in that which he differs, so guide me in that which I differ from the truth, by Your permission. Indeed, You guide whomsoever You please, to a Path which is straight." (Saheeh Muslim: 770)

(Majmoo'ul Fataawaa: 4 39)

Notes

"Verily you have in the Messenger of Allaah the best example for whoever desires Allaah and the Hereafter and who remembers Allaah often."-(Surah al-Ahzaab: 21)

Notes

"And woe to those who associate others with Allah - Those who do come with zakaat, and in disbelieve in the Hereafter.". -(Surah Fussilat: 6-7) Ibn Qayyim, may Allah Allah have mercy upon him says in Ighaathat, " The majority of early explainers of the Qur'aan and those commentators who came after them, say that the word zakaat in this verse means tawheed the testimony that there is none worthy of worship except Allaah. Beleif in it- is that by which the heart is purified."

Notes

Rajab 27th

Rajab

28th

The Prophet, may Allaah's praise and salutations be upon him, , "The difference between the one who remembers his Lord and the one who does not is like the difference between the living and the dead." (Saheeh al-Bukhaaree: 11 208)

Notes

"Purification of the soul is more difficult and harder that curing one's physical body. Whoever attempts to purify his soul through invented spiritual exercises, struggles, and seclusion which the messengers never taught is like a physically sick person who tries to cure himself based upon his personal opinion."
(Ibn Qayyim, Madaarij al-Salakeen)

Rajab
29th

Notes

Rajab

30th

«Whoever hopes in meeting his Lord, let him work righteousness, and, in the worship of his Lord, admit no one as partner.» -(Surah al-Kahf: 110)

Notes

...an extra journal page

Rajab

Notes

Sha'baan

1438

APR / MAY 2017

Yaum al-Sabt Saturday	Yaum al-Ahad Sunday	Yaum al-Ithnayn Monday	Yaum ath-Thulatha Tuesday	Yaum al-Arbi'a Wednesday	Yaum al-Khamees Thursday	Yaum al-Jumu'ah Friday
					1 27	2 28
3 29	4 30	5 1	6 2	7 3	8 4	9 5
10 6	11 7	12 8	13 9	14 10	15 11	16 12
17 13	18 14	19 15	20 16	21 17	22 18	23 19
24 20	25 21	26 22	27 23	28 24	29 25	30 26

"This is the realm of the consequences of deciding to sin: lack of success, corruption of one's perspective, the disappearance of the truth, corruption of the heart, laziness in remembrance, the loss of one's time, the people turning away from one, the estrangement between the worshiper and his Lord, the preventing of his Lord responding to his supplications, the hardening of his heart, the extermination or wiping out of Allaah's blessings in his wealth and time, the stripping away of knowledge, having humiliation placed upon him and the insult coming from his enemies, the constriction of one's heart, an increase in worthless associates, one's life becoming miserable, the mind becoming darkened- these all result from committing sins and being neglectful of the remembrance of Allaah, just as a crop grows with water but is destroyed by fire. The opposite of these are those things which are born from obedience to Allaah."

(Sheikh al-Islaam Ibn Qayyim in his work "al-Fawaid", page 34)

Abu Hurairah reported that the Messenger of Allaah, may Allaah's praise and salutations be upon him, said, "A man who is known for his good character has the same degree as someone who stands at night in prayer."
(Authenticated by Sheikh Al-Albaanee in Saheeh 'Adab al-Mufrad: 217)

Notes

"And marry those among you who are single and also marry the pious, fit and capable ones of your male slaves and female slaves. If they be poor, Allaah will enrich them out of His bounty. And Allaah is All-Sufficient for His creatures' needs, All-Knowing about the state of the people. And let those who find not the financial means for marriage keep themselves chaste, until Allaah enriches them of His bounty...." (Surah an-Noor:32-33)

Notes

'Abdullah Ibn az-Zubayr said, "I have never seen two women more generous than 'Aishah and Asma'. Yet their generosity was of different forms. 'Aishah used to gather various things and after they had been collected together, she would then give them to others. Asma' would not keep anything for charity for the next day but would give it without delay."
(Authenticated by Sheikh Al-Albaanee in Saheeh 'Adab al-Mufrad: 214)

Notes

Narrated Abu Hurairah: Allaah's Messenger said, "Allaah said, 'I will declare war against him who shows hostility to a pious worshipper of Mine. And the most beloved things by with which My slave comes nearer to Me, is that which I have enjoined upon him; and My slave keeps on coming closer to Me through performing prayer or doing extra deeds besides what is obligatory until I love him, so I become his sense of hearing with which he hears, and his sense of sight with which he sees, and his hand with which he grips, and his leg with which he walks; and if he asks Me, I will give him, and if he asks My protection, I will protect him; and I do not hesitate to do anything as I hesitate to take the soul of the believer, for he hates death, and I hate to disappoint him."
(Saheeh al-Bukhaaree)

Notes

Sha'baan

5th

"Love the one whom you love moderately, as perhaps one day he will be someone for whom you have hatred, and hate the one for whom you have hatred moderately, as perhaps one day he will be one whom you love."
(Authenticated by Sheikh al-Albaanee in 'Ghaayatul Maraam': 472)

Notes

Sha'baan

6th

Ahmad Ibn Hanbal said, "By Allaah, I have been given a significant endeavor in working with my soul, and I only wish to be successful in this as a sufficient achievement for me."
(Siyaar 'Alaam an-Nubala: vol. 11, page 222)

Notes

'Aishah said, "The Messenger of Allaah, may Allaah's praise and salutations be upon him, was never given a choice between two things but that he chose the easier of the two as long as it was not a wrong action. If it was a wrong action, then he was the last person to do it. The Messenger of Allaah, may Allaah's praise and salutations be upon him, never took revenge on his own behalf. But when the respect of Allaah Almighty was violated, he would take revenge on behalf of Allaah Almighty."
(Authenticated by Sheikh Al-Albaanee in Saheeh 'Adab al-Mufrad: 208)

Notes

Narrated 'Aishah: Allaah's Messenger, may Allaah's praise and salutations be upon him, said, "None will be called to account on the Day of Resurrection, but will be ruined." I said, "Oh Allaah's Messenger! Hasn't Allaah said, 'Then as for him who will be given his record in his right hand, he surely will receive an easy reckoning?

(Surah al-Inshiqaaq.7-8) Allaah's Messenger replied, "That verse means only the presentation of the accounts, but anybody whose account is actually questioned on the Day of Resurrection, will surely be punished."

(Saheeh al-Bukhaaree)

Notes

Narrated 'Adi Ibn Hatim: The Prophet said, "Protect yourself from the Fire."
He then turned his face aside as if he were looking at it, the Fire, and said
again, "Protect yourself from the Fire," and then turned his face aside as if he
were looking at it, and he said so for the third time, till we thought he was
looking at it. He then said, "Protect yourselves from the Fire, even if with one-
half of a date; and he who doesn't have even this, should do so by saying a good,
pleasant word.' (Saheeh al-Bukhaaree)

Notes

'Amr Ibn Shu'ayb reported from his grandfather that the Prophet, may Allaah's praise and salutations be upon him, said, "Shall I tell you about who among you I love the most and the one who will be seated closest to me on the Day of Rising?" The people were silent, so he repeated that two or three times. Then the people said, "Yes, Messenger of Allaah." He said, "The one among you with the best character."

(Authenticated by Sheikh Al-Albaanee in Saheeh 'Adab al-Mufrad: 206)

Notes

Narrated Anas Ibn Maalik: Allaah's Prophet, may Allaah's praise and salutations be upon him, used to say, "A disbeliever will be brought on the Day of Resurrection and will be asked, 'Suppose you had as much gold as to fill the earth, would you offer it to ransom yourself?' He will reply, 'Yes.' Then it will be said to him, 'You were asked for something easier than that- to join nothing in worship with Allaah, but you refused.'" (Saheeh al-Bukhaaree)

Notes

Abu Hurairah reported that the people said, "Messenger of Allaah, you joke with us!" He replied, "But I only speak the truth."
(Authenticated by Sheikh Al-Albaanee in Saheeh 'Adab al-Mufrad: 200)

Notes

"If you avoid the great sins which you are forbidden to do, We shall expiate from you your small sins, and admit you to a Noble Entrance -Paradise. And wish not for the things in which Allaah has made some of you to excel others. For men there is reward for what they have earned, and likewise for women there is reward for what they have earned, and ask Allaah of His bounty. Surely, Allaah is Ever All-Knower of everything." (Surah an-Nisaa:31-32)

Notes

Abu Hurairah would sometimes narrate about the Prophet saying, "He had a noble way of facing others. When he faced someone, he faced him completely. When he turned away, he turned away completely. I have never seen anyone like him and I will never see anyone like him."
(Authenticated by Sheikh Al-Albaanee in Saheeh 'Adab al-Mufrad: 192)

Notes

Narrated 'Aishah: Allaah's Messenger, may Allaah's praise and salutations be upon him, said, "The people will be gathered barefoot, naked, and uncircumcised." I said, "Oh Allaah's Messenger! Will the men and the women look at each other?" He said, "The situation will be too severe for them to pay any attention to that."   (Saheeh al-Bukhaaree)

Sha'baan
15th

Notes

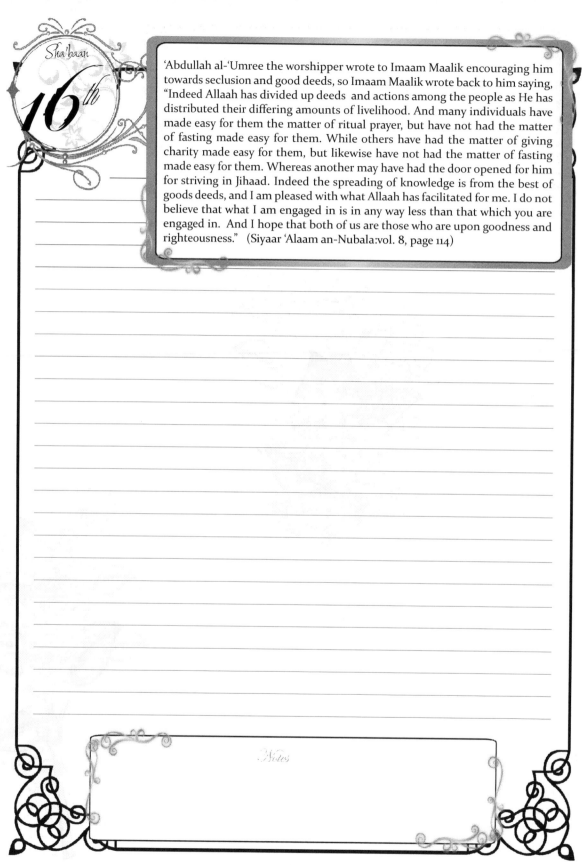

'Abdullah al-'Umree the worshipper wrote to Imaam Maalik encouraging him towards seclusion and good deeds, so Imaam Maalik wrote back to him saying, "Indeed Allaah has divided up deeds and actions among the people as He has distributed their differing amounts of livelihood. And many individuals have made easy for them the matter of ritual prayer, but have not had the matter of fasting made easy for them. While others have had the matter of giving charity made easy for them, but likewise have not had the matter of fasting made easy for them. Whereas another may have had the door opened for him for striving in Jihaad. Indeed the spreading of knowledge is from the best of goods deeds, and I am pleased with what Allaah has facilitated for me. I do not believe that what I am engaged in is in any way less than that which you are engaged in. And I hope that both of us are those who are upon goodness and righteousness." (Siyaar 'Alaam an-Nubala:vol. 8, page 114)

Notes

Abu Hurairah reported that the Prophet, may Allaah's praise and salutations be upon him, said, "Laugh little. Much laughter kills the heart." (Authenticated by Sheikh Al-Albaanee in Saheeh 'Adab al-Mufrad: 190)

Notes

Narrated Abu Hurairah: Allaah's Messenger, may Allaah's praise and salutations be upon him, said, "Whoever has wronged his brother, should ask for his pardon before his death, as in the Hereafter there will be neither a Dinar nor a Dirham. He should secure pardon in this life before some of his good deeds are taken and paid to his brother, or, if he has done no good deeds, some of the bad deeds of his brother are taken to be loaded on him in the Hereafter." (Saheeh al-Bukhaaree)

Notes

Narrated Abu Hurairah: The Prophet, may Allaah's praise and salutations be upon him, said, "Charity is obligatory everyday on every joint of a human being. If one helps a person in matters concerning his riding animal by helping him to ride it or by lifting his luggage onto it, all this will be regarded charity. A good word, and every step one takes to offer the compulsory congregational prayer, is regarded as charity; and guiding somebody on the road is regarded as charity."
(Saheeh al-Bukhaaree)

Notes

Sha'baan

20th

'Abdullah Ibn az-Zubayr said on the minbar, "Make allowances for people and command what is right and turn away from the ignorant." (Surah al-A'raaf:199) He said, "By Allaah, we are only commanded by this verse to accept people's harmful character. By Allaah, I will endure people's harmful character as long as I am with them."
(Authenticated by Sheikh Al-Albaanee in Saheeh 'Adab al-Mufrad: 184)

Notes

As-Sha'bee said, "What these people speak to you about- then if it is from the Prophet, may Allaah's praise and salutations be upon him, then take it, and what they speak about from their opinion then, meet it with a cutting blade to weed through it."
(Siyaar 'Alaam an-Nubala: vol. 4, page 80)

Notes

"And when Our Clear Verses are recited to them, they say, 'This is nothing but a man who wishes to hinder you from that which your fathers used to worship.' And they say, 'This Qur'an is nothing but an invented lie.' And those who disbelieve say of the truth when it has come to them- Prophet Muhammad- when Allaah sent him as a Messenger with proofs, evidences, verses of this Qur'an, 'This is nothing but evident magic!' (Surah as-Sabaa:043)

Notes

Abu Hurairah said, "A believer is the mirror of his brother. When he sees a fault in it, he should correct it."
(Authenticated by Sheikh Al-Albaanee in Saheeh 'Adab al-Mufrad: 177)

Notes

'Amr Ibn Maymoon said, "If I came to learn that there was a single letter of the Sunnah that I did not possess that remained down in Yemen, then I would go after it." Imaam ad-Dhahabee said, "This assertion is an indication of the extensiveness of his knowledge."
(Siyaar 'Alaam an-Nubala: vol. 6, page 346)

Notes

'Abdullah Ibn al-Khatami reported that the Messenger of Allaah, may Allaah's praise and salutations be upon him, said, "Every good action is charity." (Authenticated by Sheikh Al-Albaanee in Saheeh 'Adab al-Mufrad: 171)

Notes

265

Sha'baan

26th

Umm Musa said, "I heard 'Ali say that the Prophet, may Allaah's praise and salutations be upon him, commanded 'Abdullah Ibn Mas'ud to climb a tree and bring him something from it. His Companions looked at 'Abdullah's thigh and laughed at its leaness. The Messenger of Allaah, may Allaah's praise and salutations be upon him, said, 'Why are you laughing? This man Abdullah's foot is heavier in the balance than the mountain of Uhud.'"
(Authenticated by Sheikh Al-Albaanee in Saheeh 'Adab al-Mufrad: 176)

Notes

Narrated Anas Ibn Malik: The Prophet said, "Allaah will say to the person who will have the minimum punishment in the Fire on the Day of Resurrection, 'If you had things equal to whatever is on the earth, would you ransom yourself from the punishment with it?' He will reply, 'Yes.' Allaah will say, 'I asked you a much easier thing than this while you were in the backbone of Adam- that is, not to worship others besides Me, but you refused and insisted on worshipping others besides Me.'" (Saheeh al-Bukhaaree)

Notes

Sha'baan
28th

Qabisa Ibn Burma al-Asadi said, "I was with the Messenger of Allaah, may Allaah's praise and salutations be upon him, and I heard him say, 'The people of doing what is good in this world are the people of good in the Hereafter. The people of the wrongdoing in this world are the people of the wrongdoing in the Hereafter.'"
(Authenticated by Sheikh Al-Albaanee in Saheeh 'Adab al-Mufrad:)

Notes

Abu Musa reported that the Prophet, may Allaah's praise and salutations be upon him, said, "Every Muslim must give charity." They said, "And if he does not find anything (to give)?" He replied, "Then he should work with his hands, benefit himself and then give charity." They asked, "And if he is unable to or does not do it?" He replied, "Then he should help someone with a great need." They said, "And if he does not do it?" He replied, "Then he should command the good or command that which is correct." They said, "And if he does not do that?" They said, "He should refrain from evil. That is charity for him."
(Authenticated by Sheikh Al-Albaanee in Saheeh 'Adab al-Mufrad: 166)

Notes

Sha'baan

30th

Narrated Anas Ibn Malik: The Prophet, may Allaah's praise and salutations be upon him, said, "Some people will come out of the Hellfire after they have received a touch of the Fire, changing their color, and they will enter Paradise, and the people of Paradise will name them, 'Al-Jahannamiyin'- the Hellfire people." (Saheeh al-Bukhaaree)

Notes

Sha'baan

...an extra journal page

Notes

Ramadhaan

1438

MAY / JUN 2017

Yaum al-Sabt Saturday	Yaum al-Ahad Sunday	Yaum al-Ithnayn Monday	Yaum ath-Thulatha Tuesday	Yaum al-Arba'a Wednesday	Yaum al-Khamees Thursday	Yaum al-Jumu'ah Friday
1 27	2 28	3 29	4 30	5 31	6 1	7 2
8 3	9 4	10 5	11 6	12 7	13 8	14 9
15 10	16 11	17 12	18 13	19 14	20 15	21 16
22 17	23 18	24 19	25 20	26 21	27 22	28 23
29	*30					

"-If you expose your sight to what is impermissible, then know this is like entering into a battle; so seek your protection behind a shield. As Allaah says, "Tell the believing men to lower their gaze..." Such that then they are protected from the assault of negative effects. And He says, "Allaah suffices for the believers in the fighting."

-The sea of one's desires is one he can easily drown within- yet the one swimming down in its depths is afraid to even open his eyes!

-How many people try to gather their pleasures in this world before it is the time of their proper time of harvest! Do not falsely believe that this world is when the fruits will truly be ripe.

-Purchase your soul now, in this world, while the market is open and the charge or price is still available to you."

(Sheikh al-Islaam Ibn Qayyim in his work "al-Fawaid", page 41)

Anas reported that the Muhaajiroon said, "Messenger of Allaah, the Ansar have taken all the reward!" He said, "No, not as long as you make supplication for them and praise them for it."
(Authenticated by Sheikh Al-Albaanee in Saheeh 'Adab al-Mufrad: 159)

Notes:

From 'Ikrimah from Ibn 'Abbaas who said: "Narrate to the people once every week; and if you cannot accept this, then twice; and if you do it a abundantly- then three times. And do not make the people fed up with this Qur'an and do not come to a people when they are speaking with some of their general talk such that you start to relate to them and cut off their talk and therefore bore them, but simply remain silent. So when they then ask you then to narrate to them, such that they are eager; and avoid rhymed prose when making supplication. Because I experienced that Messenger of Allaah, may Allaah's praise and salutations be upon him, and his Companions did not do this; rather they only avoided it." (Saheeh al-Bukhaaree: 349)

Notes

Narrated Usama: The Prophet, may Allaah's praise and salutations be upon him, said, "I stood at the gate of Paradise and saw that the majority of the people who had entered it were poor people, while the rich were forbidden to enter along with the poor, because they were waiting the reckoning of their accounts; but the people of the Fire had been ordered to be driven to the Fire. And I stood at the gate of the Fire and found that the majority of the people entering it were women." (Saheeh al-Bukhaaree)

Ramadhaan
3rd

Notes

Jabir Ibn 'Abdullah al-Ansari reported that the Prophet, may Allaah's praise and salutations be upon him, said, "Whoever has a favor done for him should repay it. If he cannot find anything he can use to repay it, he should praise the one who did it. When he praises him, he thanks him. If he is silent, he is ungrateful to him. If someone adorns himself with something he has not been given, it is as if he was wearing a false garment."
(Authenticated by Sheikh Al-Albaanee in Saheeh 'Adab al-Mufrad: 157)

Notes

" He it is Who sent down calmness and tranquility into the hearts of the believers, that they may grow more in faith along with their present faith. And to Allaah belong the hosts of the heavens and the earth, and Allaah is Ever All-Knower, All-Wise. That He may admit the believing men and the believing women to Gardens under which rivers flow –Paradise- to abide therein forever, and He may expiate from them their sins; and that is with Allaah a supreme success And that He may punish the hypocrites men and women, and also the men and women who associate others with Allaah in worship, who think evil thoughts about Allaah, for them is a disgraceful torment. And the Anger of Allaah is upon them, and He has cursed them and prepared Hell for them – and worst indeed is that destination.
(Surah al-Fath:4-6)

Notes:

Ramadhaan

6th

Abu Sulayman Malik Ibn al-Huwayrith said, "We came to the Prophet, may Allaah's praise and salutations be upon him, being young men of a similar age. We spent twenty nights with him. He thought that we desired our own people and he asked us about those of our family we had left behind, and we told him. He was merciful and kind, and said, 'Go back to your family. Instruct and command them. Pray as you have seen me praying. When it is time for the prayer, then let one of you give the adhan and let the oldest of you lead the prayer.'"
(Authenticated by Sheikh Al-Albaanee in Saheeh 'Adab al-Mufrad: 156)

Notes

"Oh Ever Living, Oh Self-Subsisting and Supporter of all, by Your mercy I seek assistance. Rectify for me all of my affairs and do not leave me to myself, even for the blink of an eye." (Authenticated by Sheikh Al-Albaanee in Saheeh at-Targheeb wa at-Tarheeb 1 273)

Notes

Ramadhaan
8th

Abu Hurairah said, "The Prophet, may Allaah's praise and salutations be upon him, was asked, 'Messenger of Allaah! A certain woman prays in the night, fasts in the day, acts and gives charity, but injures her neighbors with her tongue.' The Messenger of Allaah, may Allaah's praise and salutations be upon him, said, 'There is no good in her. She is one of the people of the Fire.' They said, 'Another woman prays the prescribed prayers and gives bits of curd as charity and does not injure anyone.' The Messenger of Allaah, may Allaah's praise and salutations be upon him, said, 'She is one of the people of the Garden.'"
(Authenticated by Sheikh Al-Albaanee in Saheeh 'Adab al-Mufrad: 88)

Notes

'Oh Allaah, You are my supporter and You are my helper, by You I move and by You I attack and by You I battle.'
(Collected in Saheeh at-Tirmidhee 1 77)

Ramadhaan
10th

Al-Awzaa'aee said, "Hold firmly to the transmissions from the first generations even if the people reject you, and be warned away from the opinion of men, despite them beautifying them for you with their speech. As this way is evident and clear and upon it you stand upon the straight path."
(Siyaar 'Alaam an-Nubala: vol. 7, page 120)

Notes

Mujaahid reported that a sheep was slaughtered for 'Abdullah Ibn 'Amr. He asked his slave, "Have you given any to our Jewish neighbor? Have you given any to our Jewish neighbor? As I heard the Messenger of Allaah, may Allaah's praise and salutations be upon him, say, 'Jibreel kept on enjoining upon me that I treat my neighbors well until I thought that he would order me to treat them as my heirs.'"
(Authenticated by Sheikh Al-Albaanee in Saheeh 'Adab al-Mufrad: 78)

Notes

Narrated Abu Hazim from Sahl Ibn Sa'd: The Prophet said, "I am your predecessor at the Hawdh, or lake, and whoever will pass by there, he will drink from it, and whoever will drink from it, he will never be thirsty. There will come to me some people whom I will recognize, and they will recognize me, but a barrier will be placed between me and them." Abu Hazim added: An-Nu'man Ibn Abi 'Aiyash, on hearing me, said, "Did you hear this from Sahl?" I said, "Yes." He said, " I bear witness that I heard Abu Said Al-Khudri saying the same, adding that the Prophet, may Allaah's praise and salutations be upon him, said, 'I will say: They are my followers. It will be said, 'You do not know what they innovated of new things in the religion after you left'. I will say, 'Far removed, far removed from mercy, those who changed their religion after me.'" Abu Hurairah narrated that the Prophet, may Allaah's praise and salutations be upon him, said, "On the Day of Resurrection a group of companions will come to me, but will be driven away from the Hawdh, and I will say, 'Oh Lord those are my companions!' It will be said, 'You have no knowledge as to what they innovated after you left; they turned apostate as renegades and reverted from Islaam." (Saheeh al-Bukhaaree)

Notes

Ramadhaan 13th

"And in the alternation of night and day, and the provision of rain that Allaah sends down from the sky, and revives therewith the earth after its death, and in the turning about of the winds -sometimes towards the east or north, and sometimes towards the south or west, sometimes bringing glad tidings of rain and sometimes bringing the torment, are signs for a people who understand." (Surah al-Jaathiyah: 5)

Notes:

Sufyaan at-Thawree said, "I have never been informed of a practice of the Messenger of Allaah, may Allaah's praise and salutations be upon him, except that I acted upon it, even if only once."
(Siyaar 'Alaam an-Nubala: vol. 7, page 242)

Notes

'Aishah said, "A bedouin came to the Prophet, may Allaah's praise and salutations be upon him, and asked, 'Do you kiss your children? We do not kiss them.' The Prophet, may Allaah's praise and salutations be upon him, said, 'Can I put mercy in your hearts after Allaah has removed it from them?'" (Authenticated by Sheikh Al-Albaanee in Saheeh 'Adab al-Mufrad: 90)

Notes

"And tell the believing women to lower their gaze from looking at forbidden things, and protect their private parts from illegal sexual acts and not to show off their adornment except that which is apparent and to draw their veils all over their bodies, faces, necks and bosoms and not to reveal their adornment except to their husbands, or their fathers, or their husband's fathers, or their sons, or their husband's sons, or their brothers or their brother's sons, or their sister's sons, or their women , or the female slaves whom their right hands possess, or old male servants who lack vigor, or small children who have no sense of feminine sex. And let them not stamp their feet so as to reveal what they hide of their adornment. And all of you beg Allaah to forgive you all, Oh believers, that you may be successful."   (Surah an-Noor: 31)

Notes

'Abdullah Ibn al-Mubarak said, "Make your foundational pillar those transmitted narrations, and thereafter take from opinions that which explains for you those hadeeth narrations."
(Siyaar 'Alaam an-Nubala: vol. 8, page 241)

Notes

Anas said, "One day I visited the Prophet, may Allaah's praise and salutations be upon him, and there was only myself, my mother and my aunt, Umm Hiram. When he came to us, he asked us, 'Shall I pray with you?' It was not the time of an obligatory prayer." One of those listening to the person relating this asked, "Where did he put Anas in relation to himself?" The reply was, "He put him to his right." The report from Anas continues, "Then he prayed with us and made supplication for us, the people of the house, that we would have the best of the blessings of this world and the Next. My mother said, 'Messenger of Allaah, make supplication to Allaah for your little servant,' and he asked Allaah to grant me every blessing. At the end of his supplication, he said, 'Oh Allaah, grant him abundant wealth and many children and bless him!'"
(Authenticated by Sheikh Al-Albaanee in Saheeh 'Adab al-Mufrad: 88)

Notes

Muhammad Ibn Salaam al-Baykindee said, I heard Walee'a say, "The one who seek to learn hadeeths to take from their guidance as it comes, then he is an individual upon the Sunnah, and the one who seeks to learn them simply to strengthen his opinion, then he is an individual upon innovation in the religion."
(Siyaar 'Alaam an-Nubala: vol. 9, page 144)

Notes

Narrated Abu Hurairah: I said, "Oh Allaah's Messenger! Who will be the most fortunate person who will gain your intercession on the Day of Resurrection?" The Prophet, may Allaah's praise and salutations be upon him, said, "Oh Abu Hurairah! I have thought that none will ask me about this hadeeth before you, as I know your longing for the learning of hadeeths. The most fortunate person who will have my intercession on the Day of Resurrection will be the one who said, 'None has the right to be worshipped but Allaah,' sincerely from the bottom of his heart.'" (Saheeh al-Bukhaaree)

Notes

Jabir Ibn 'Abdullah reported that the Messenger of Allaah, may Allaah's praise and salutations be upon him, said, "Anyone who has three daughters and provides for them, clothes them and shows mercy to them will definitely enter the Garden." A man from the people said, "And two daughters, Messenger of Allaah?" He said, "And two."
(Authenticated by Sheikh Al-Albaanee in Saheeh 'Adab al-Mufrad: 78)

Ramadhaan

21st

Notes

"Men are the protectors and maintainers of women, because Allaah has made one of them to excel the other, and because they spend to support them from their means. Therefore the righteous women are devoutly obedient to Allaah and to their husbands, and guard in the husband's absence what Allaah orders them to guard -their chastity and their husband's property".
(Surah an-Nisaa:034)

Notes

Ar-Rabee said a man asked Imaam Shaafa'ee, "Do you accept and take from this hadeeth, Abu 'Abdullah?" So he replied, "When an authentic hadeeth is narrated from the Messenger of Allaah, may Allaah's praise and salutation be upon him, and I do not take it- then you will have witnessed that I have then lost my mind."
(Siyaar 'Alaam an-Nubala: vol. 10, page 34)

Notes

"So that Allaah will punish the hypocrites, men and women, and the men and women who are those who associate others in the worship of Allaah. And Allaah will pardon or accept the repentance of the true believers, men and women. And Allaah is Ever Oft-Forgiving, Most Merciful."
(Surah al-Ahzaab:073)

Notes

Abu Thawr said that he heard Imaam Shaafa'ee say "Every hadeeth truly from the Prophet, may Allaah's praise and salutations be upon him- that is my statement also, even if you have never heard me state it."
(Siyaar 'Alaam an-Nubala: vol. 10, page 35)

Notes

The Messenger of Allaah, may Allaah's praise and salutations be upon him, said, "We are an illiterate nation. We do not use astronomical writing or computation in our fasting. A month is so and so and so" and he pointed with his hands three times, folding the thumb on the third time- meaning twenty nine days-"or so and so and so", and he pointed with his hands three times- meaning thirty days. (Saheeh al-Bukhaaree, Saheeh Muslim and others)

Notes

Hakeem Ibn Hizam said to the Prophet, may Allaah's praise and salutations be upon him, "Do you think that the acts of worship which I used to do in the time of the Jahiliyyah – maintaining relations with relatives, setting slaves fre, and charity – will bring me a reward?" Hakeem said that the Messenger of Allaah, may Allaah's praise and salutations be upon him, said, "When you become Muslim, you keep the good actions you have already done." (Authenticated by Sheikh Al-Albaanee in Saheeh 'Adab al-Mufrad: 70)

Notes

"But they have broken their religion among them into sects, each group rejoicing in what is with it as its beliefs. And every party is pleased with whatever they stand with." –(Surah al-Mu'minoon: 53)

Notes

Abu Sulaymaan ad-Daaraanee said, "Sometimes there occurs in my heart a saying from the saying of the people of today, yet I do not accept it except when supported by two upright witnesses; they are the Book of Allaah and the Sunnah." (Siyaar 'Alaam an-Nubala: vol. 10, page 183)

Ramadhaan 29th

Notes

301

Al-Bara' said, "A Bedouin came and said, 'Prophet of Allaah! Teach me an action which will enable me to enter the Garden.' He said, 'The question is a broad one, even though you have asked it in only a few words. Free someone. Set a slave free.' He said, 'Are they not the same thing?' 'No,' he replied, 'Freeing someone is setting someone free yourself. Setting a slave free is to contribute to the price of setting him free. Lend an animal for milking which has a lot of milk and treat your relatives kindly. If you cannot do that, then command the good and forbid the bad. If you cannot do that, then restrain your tongue from everything except what is good.'"
(Authenticated by Sheikh Al-Albaanee in Saheeh 'Adab al-Mufrad: 69)

Notes

...an extra journal page

Ramadhaan

Notes

Shawwal

1438

JUN / JUL 2017

Yaum al-Sabt Saturday	Yaum al-Ahad Sunday	Yaum al-Ithnayn Monday	Yaum ath-Thulatha Tuesday	Yaum al-Arbi'a Wednesday	Yaum al-Khamees Thursday	Yaum al-Jumi'ah Friday
	1 25	2 26	3 27	4 28	5 29	6 30
7 1	8 2	9 3	10 4	11 5	12 6	13 7
14 8	15 9	16 10	17 11	18 12	19 13	20 14
21 15	22 16	23 17	24 18	25 19	26 20	27 21
28 22	29 23					

"-It is unavoidable that one occasionally slip into the sleep of following desires and some heedlessness, but sleep lightly! As the watchman is announcing that the morning of the Hereafter has almost arrived.

-The light of a sound intellect helps illuminate through the night of our desires, indicating the road towards what is correct. It grants one perspective and insight, such that one is able to discern the true consequences of various matters."

(Sheikh al-Islaam Ibn Qayyim in his work *"al-Fawaid"*, page 41)

"Verily, it is the party of Allaah that will be the successful."
(Surah al-Mujadilaah: 58).

Shawwal
1st

Notes

Imaam Ahmad Ibn Hanbal said, "The one who rejects a hadeeth of the Messenger of Allaah, may Allaah's praise and salutations be upon him, he stands on the point of destruction."
(Siyaar 'Alaam an-Nubala: vol. 10, page 297)

Notes

It is reported that al-Miqdam Ibn Ma'dikarib heard the Messenger of Allaah, may Allaah's praise and salutations be upon him, say, "Allaah enjoins you to be dutiful to your mothers. Then He enjoins you to be dutiful to your mothers. Then He enjoins you to be dutiful to your fathers. Then He enjoins you to be dutiful to your next closest relative and then to your next closest relative." (Authenticated by Sheikh Al-Albaanee in Saheeh 'Adab al-Mufrad: 60)

Notes

Shawwal

4th

"And verily, this is my straight path, so follow it, and follow not other paths, for they will separate you away from His path. This He has ordained for you that you may become pious." (Surah al-An'aam:153)

Notes

Ibn 'Umar said, "If someone fears his Lord and maintains ties of kinship, his term of life will be prolonged, he will have abundant wealth, and his people will love him."
(Authenticated by Sheikh Al-Albaanee in Saheeh 'Adab al-Mufrad: 58)

Shawwal
5th

Notes

Shawwal

6th

Abu Hilal said, Qatadah was asked about an issue and he replied, "I don't know." It was said, "Speak according to what your opinion is." He replied, "I have not spoken according to my opinion in over forty years." And at that time he was fifty years old. Imaam ad-Dhahabee said, "This indicates that he did not ever speak in matters of knowledge simply from his opinions." (Siyaar 'Alaam an-Nubala: vol. 5, page 273)

Notes

"And remember when the angels said, 'Oh Maryam! Verily, Allaah has chosen you, purified you from polytheism and disbelief, and chosen you above the women of the worlds. Oh Maryam! Submit yourself with obedience to your Lord and prostrate yourself, and bow down along with those who bow down.' This is a part of the news of the unseen, i.e. the news of the past nations of which you have no knowledge which We reveal to you. You were not with them, when they cast lots with their pens as to which of them should be charged with the care of Maryam; nor were you with them when they disputed."
(Surah Aal-'Imraan:42-44)

Notes

Anas Ibn Maalik reported that the Messenger of Allaah, may Allaah's praise and salutations be upon him, said, "Anyone who wants to have his provision expanded and his term of life prolonged should maintain ties of kinship." (Authenticated by Sheikh Al-Albaanee in Saheeh 'Adab al-Mufrad: 56)

Notes

'Abdullah Ibn Muslim al-Marooze said, "I used to sit with Ibn Sirreen, and once I sat with the people from the sect of the Ibaadheeyah, and I came to see that I was sitting with a people whom it was as if they were carrying forth to put the Prophet, may Allaah praise and salutations be upon him, in the ground. Then later I came to Ibn Sirreen and mentioned this to him and he said, 'What is wrong with you that you would sit with a people who wish to place in a grave that guidance which the Messenger of Allaah came with?!'" (Siyaar 'Alaam an-Nubala: vol. 4, page 617)

Notes

"The one who associates others in his worship with Allaah takes as partners and rivals others besides Allaah, loving them as only Allaah should be loved. Whereas the one who singles out Allaah alone in worship loves who he loves only for the sake of Allaah, and he hates whoever Allaah hates for Allaah's sake alone. He engages in any deed or action for Allaah's sake alone and he turns away from whatever he turns away from for Allaah's sake alone. The true realm of this religion is based upon these four mentioned principles: one's love and one's hate, and based upon these two are those matters that you engage in and undertake, those which you turn away from and abandon, those related to what you give and offer to others, and those related to what you withhold and keep back from them. As such, the one who completes and fulfils what is required by these four related principles, completes his faith, and the one who has deficiencies within their implementation is reckoned as a worshiper with deficiencies within his faith."

(A Treatise Written by Ibn Qayyim to One of His Brothers , page 36)

Notes

Ibn 'Umar reported that the Messenger of Allaah, may Allaah's praise and salutations be upon him, said, "The strongest form of dutifulness is when a man maintains relations with the people his father loved."
(Authenticated by Sheikh Al-Albaanee in Saheeh 'Adab al-Mufrad: 41)

Notes

"Oh you who believe! Let not a group ridicule at another group, as it may be that the latter are better than the former. Nor let some women ridicule at other women, as it may be that the latter are better than the former. Nor defame one another, nor insult one another by nicknames. How bad is it to insult one's brother after having faith. And whosoever does not repent, then such are indeed wrong doers." (Surah al-Hujuraat: 11)

Notes

Imaam Maalik said, "Every time some argumentative man comes to us, are we to abandon that guidance which was sent down with Jibreel to Muhammad, may Allaah's praise and salutations be upon him, due to his arguments??" (Siyaar 'Alaam an-Nubala: vol. 8, page 99)

Shawwal

13th

Notes

Abu Hurairah said, "Neither Jew nor Christian has heard me and then not loved me. I wanted my mother to become Muslim, but she refused. I told her about it and she still refused. I went to the Prophet, may Allaah's praise and salutations be upon him, and said, 'Pray to Allaah for me.' He did so and I went to her. She was inside the door of the house and said, 'Abu Hurairah, I have become Muslim.' I told the Prophet, may Allaah's praise and salutations be upon him, and I asked, 'Make supplication to Allaah for me and my mother.' He said, 'Oh Allaah, make people love Abu Hurairah and his mother.'"

(Authenticated by Sheikh Al-Albaanee in Saheeh 'Adab al-Mufrad: 34)

Notes

"As for those who strive hard with regard to Us - in Our Cause, We will surely guide them to Our Paths - Allaah's Religion. Verily, Allaah is with the good doers." (Surah Al-Ankabut: 69)

Notes

Shawwal 16th

Imaam Shaafa'ee said that whenever some of those people who followed their desires would come to Imaam Maalik to debate he would say, "As for me I stand upon clarity from my Lord, but as for you who are upon doubt, then go find someone like you upon doubt, and dispute with him."
(Siyaar 'Alaam an-Nubala: vol. 8, page 99)

Notes

Abu Hurairah reported that the Prophet, may Allaah's praise and salutations be upon him, said, "May he be disgraced, may he be disgraced, may he be disgraced!" They said, "Oh Messenger of Allaah, who?" He replied, "The one who fails both of his parents, or even one of them, when they become old, will enter the Fire."
(Authenticated by Sheikh Al-Albaanee in Saheeh 'Adab al-Mufrad: 16)

Notes

Abu Hurairah reported that the Prophet, may Allaah's praise and salutations be upon him, said, "Three supplications are without a doubt answered: the supplication of someone who is oppressed, the supplication of someone on a journey, and the supplication of parents for their children."
(Authenticated by Sheikh Al-Albaanee in Saheeh 'Adab al-Mufrad: 32)

Notes

"Where so ever you may be, death will overtake you even if you are in fortresses built up strong and high!" And if some good reaches them, they say, 'This is from Allaah,' but if some evil befalls them, they say, 'This is from you.' Say, 'All things are from Allaah,' so what is wrong with these people that they fail to understand any word? Whatever of good reaches you, is from Allaah, but whatever of evil befalls you, is from yourself. And We have sent you -Oh Muhammad - as a Messenger to mankind, and Allaah is Sufficient as a Witness." (Surah an-Nisaa:78-79)

Notes

Shawwal 20th

The Companions of the Messenger of Allaah, may Allaah's praise and salutations be upon him, mentioned this world one day in his presence, so the Messenger of Allaah said, "Will you not listen, will you not listen! Wearing old clothes is part of imaan, wearing old clothes is part of imaan!"
(Authenticated by Sheikh al-Albaanee - Sunan Abu Dawood: 4149)

Notes

Abu ad-Darda' said, "The Messenger of Allaah, may Allaah's praise and salutations be upon him, counseled me with nine matters: 'Do not associate anything with Allaah, even if due to this you are cut into pieces or burned alive. Do not intentionally leave any of the obligatory prayers. Anyone who intentionally does so loses Allaah's protection. Do not drink wine, as it is a key to opening every evil. Obey both your parents, and if they order you to spend from your wealth, then spend upon them. Do not enter into conflict and opposition with the rulers, even if you think that you stand upon the truth. Do not run away from the enemy army when it comes forward, even if your companions run away and you end up being killed. Spend from your means on your wife, and do not raise your stick to hit her. And cause your family to fear Allaah, the Almighty and Exalted.'"
(Authenticated by Sheikh Al-Albaanee in Saheeh 'Adab al-Mufrad: 18)

Notes

Sa'eed Ibn Jubayr said, "Having fear of Allaah is that you fear Allaah such that you place your fear between you and your sins. This is truly having the fear of Allaah. And remembering Allaah is obeying him, as the one who obeys Allaah recalls and remembers him, and the one who does not obey Him does not remember Him, even he is one who says subhaanallaah often and frequently recites the Qur'an."
(Siyaar 'Alaam an-Nubala: vol. 4, page 326)

Notes

Maymoon said, "I once visited Ibn 'Umar, and judged that everything contained within his house of furnishings was equal to the value of one hundred dirhams." (Siyaar 'Alaam an-Nubala: vol. 3, page 213)

Shawwal
23rd

Notes

Abu't-Tufayl said, "'Alee was asked, 'Did the Prophet, may Allaah's praise and salutations be upon him, give you something specific, which he did not give to anyone else?' He replied, 'The Messenger of Allaah, may Allaah's praise and salutations be upon him, did not convey to me anything specific which he did not give to all others except for what I keep within the scabbard of my sword.' He brought out a page upon which was written: 'Allaah curses anyone who sacrifices an animal for any other than Allaah alone. Allaah curses anyone who steals a road marker which guides travelers. Allaah curses anyone who curses his parents. And Allaah curses anyone who gives shelter to the ones who bring new matters into the religion.'"
(Authenticated by Sheikh Al-Albaanee in Saheeh 'Adab al-Mufrad: 13)

Notes

"And many from amongst the Prophets fought (in Allaah's cause) and along with him fought large bands of religious learned men. But they never lost heart for that which did befall them in Allaah's way, nor did they weaken nor degrade themselves. And Allaah loves those who are patient. And they said nothing but, 'Our Lord! Forgive us our sins and our transgressions in keeping our duties to You, establish our feet firmly, and give us victory over the disbelieving people.' So Allaah gave them the reward of this world, and the excellent reward of the Hereafter. And Allaah loves the good-doers."
(Surah Aal-'Imraan:146-148)

Notes

Shawwal

26th

Abee Bakarah related that the Messenger of Allaah, may Allaah's praise and salutations be upon him, said, "Should I not inform you of what are the worst of the major transgressions?" repeating it three times. We replied, "Yes, of course, oh Messenger of Allaah!" He said, "To associate others with Allaah in worship, and to be disobedient to one's parents." He then sat up, as previously he had been reclining, and added "and bearing false witness." And he kept repeating this until I said to myself, "If only he would be quiet." (Authenticated by Sheikh Al-Albaanee in Saheeh 'Adab al-Mufrad: 12)

Notes

Yunus as-Sadafee said Shaafa'ee said to me, "There is no way to be completely protected from the harm of the people, so search among them for those in whom your rectification may be found and stay with them."
(Siyaar 'Alaam an-Nubala: vol. 10, page 42)

27th

Notes

Shawwal
28th

"The believers, men and women, are helpers, supporters, and protectors of one another; they enjoin on the people that which is good, and forbid people from all kinds of wrongdoing, and all that Islaam has forbidden; they perform as-Salaat- the ritual prayers- and give the zakaat- the obligatory charity- and obey Allaah and His Messenger; Allaah will have His Mercy on them. Surely, Allaah is All-Mighty, All-Wise."
(Surah at-Tawbah:071)

Notes

Abu Murra reported that the freed client of Umm Hani' Bint Abu Taalib had told him that he rode with Abu Hurairah to his homeland in al-'Aqeeq. When he entered his family's area, he called out in his loudest voice, "Peace and protection be upon you and the mercy of Allaah and His blessings! Oh mother!" She replied, "And peace and protection be upon you and the mercy of Allaah and His blessings." He said, "May Allaah have mercy on you as you raised me when I was young." She replied, "Oh my son, may Allaah reward you with goodness and be pleased with you, as you treated me with kindness when I became old."

(Authenticated by Sheikh Al-Albaanee in Saheeh 'Adab al-Mufrad: 11)

Shawwal 29th

Notes

Muhammad Ibn Musa said, I saw Abu 'Abdullah Ahmad Ibn Hanbal when a man from Khuraasaan said to him, "All praise is due to Allaah who enabled me to be able to see you." He replied, "Sit down, what is this you are saying? Who am I to deserve this?" And it is also reported that a man said, "I saw signs of distress upon the face of Abu 'Abdullah when a man praised him by saying, "Allaah has blessed Islaam with good through you." He replied, "Rather, Allaah has blessed me with the good of Islaam. Who am I, who am I?!" (Siyaar 'Alaam an-Nubala: vol. 11, page 226)

Notes

Shawwal

...an extra journal page

Notes

Dhul-Qi'ddah

1438

JUL / AUG 2017

Yaum al-Sabt Saturday	*Yaum al-Ahad* Sunday	*Yaum al-Ithnayn* Monday	*Yaum ath-Thulatha* Tuesday	*Yaum al-Arba'a* Wednesday	*Yaum al-Khamees* Thursday	*Yaum al-Jumu'ah* Friday
		1 24	2 25	3 26	4 27	5 28
6 29	7 30	8 31	9 1	10 2	11 3	12 4
13 5	14 6	15 7	16 8	17 9	18 10	19 11
20 12	21 13	22 14	23 15	24 16	25 17	26 18
27 19	28 20	29 21	30 22			

"Seek to have the determination to leave this cramped world filled with its ailments and maladies to move to that vast world of the next life which has enjoyments which no eye has seen, every desire is fulfilled, and nothing which is beloved is ever lost. Oh one who has sold yourself for a desire which offers you so little and in fact only brings you harm, and the best of which will fade away! You have bartered away the most valuable of things for the cheapest price, as if you were unaware of its preciousness as well as not understanding the meagerness of what was given in exchange! Yet on that Day of mutual loss it will become clear to you the loss in this poor deal you have made. The living the truth of "There is none worthy of worship except Allaah" is the merchandise that Allaah is purchasing, and its price to you given in exchange in Paradise, while the agent of sale of the Messenger of Allaah. So you should truly be pleased to purchase it for even a small part of this passing world which in its entirety is not even worth the wing of a single mosquito."

(Sheikh al-Islaam Ibn Qayyim in his work "al-Fawaid", page 41)

"He who emigrates from his home in the Cause of Allaah, will find on earth many dwelling places and plenty to live by. And whosoever leaves his home as an emigrant to Allaah and His Messenger, and death overtakes him, his reward is then surely incumbent upon Allaah. And Allaah is Ever Oft-Forgiving, Most Merciful." (Surah an-Nisaa:100)

Notes

Al-Husayn Ibn Ismaa'el narrated that his father said, "There would be in the gathering of Imaam Ahmad Ibn Hanbal nearly five thousand or more people, and perhaps five hundred of them would be students writing down hadeeth narrations, while the remaining people were learning from him good manners and the proper way to be." (Siyaar 'Alaam an-Nubala: vol. 11, page 316)

Notes

"And they will never cease fighting you until they turn you back from your religion if they can. And whosoever of you turns back from his religion and dies as a disbeliever, then his deeds will be lost in this life and in the Hereafter, and they will be the dwellers of the Fire. They will abide therein forever."
(Surah al-Baqarah:217)

Dhul-Qi'dah
3rd

Notes

Dhul-Qi'ddah
4th

"Whoever loves for Allaah and hates for Allaah, gives for Allaah and withholds for Allaah, then he has completed imaan."
(Authenticated by Sheikh al-Albaanee in Sunan Abu Dawud: 3664)

Notes

Al-Husayn Ibn Muhammad al-Samarqandee said, "Muhammad Ibn Isma'eel (Imaam al-Bukhaaree) was especially characterized by three attributes among everything he had of praiseworthy attributes. He spoke only a little, he did not desire what the people possessed, and he did not busy himself with the various affairs of the people; rather, he occupied himself in matters of knowledge."
(Siyaar 'Alaam an-Nubala: vol. 12, page 449)

Notes

"If you ask them about this, they declare: 'We were only talking idly and joking.' Say, "Was it at Allaah, and His verses and signs and His Messenger that you were mocking?' Make no excuse; you indeed disbelieved after you had believed. If We pardon some of you, We will punish others amongst you because they are sinners or criminals. The hypocrites, men and women, are one from another; they enjoin on the people wrongdoing, and forbid people from what is good, and they close their hands from spending in Allaah's Cause. They have forgotten Allaah, so He has forgotten them. Verily, the hypocrites are the rebellious, disobedient to Allaah."
(Surah at-Tawbah:065-67)

Notes

Abdullah Ibn 'Amr said, "A man came to the Prophet, may Allaah's praise and salutations be upon him, and made a pledge to him that he would emigrate to Medinah. When he had left his parents were in tears. The Prophet, may Allaah's praise and salutations be upon him, said, 'Return to them and make them smile, just as you made them cry.'"
(Authenticated by Sheikh Al-Albaanee in Saheeh 'Adab al-Mufrad: 10)

Notes

From Abdullah Ibn Mas'ood , may Allaah be pleased with them both, who said, "How will you be when you are covered by a trial in which the young grow up and the old become infirm. If anything of it is abandoned it is said: The Sunnah has been abandoned." It was said, "When will that occur, Oh Abu Abdur Rahman?" He said, "When your scholars pass away, and those ignorant amongst you become numerous; when those who recite amongst you are many, but those who have understanding of the religion are few; when your leaders are many, but those who are trustworthy are few; when this world is sought through the actions of the Hereafter; and when knowledge is sought for other than the Religion."
(Sunan ad-Daramee 1 64 and others)

Notes

"And whoso obeys Allaah and the Messenger, then they will be in the company of those on whom Allaah has bestowed His Grace, of the Prophets, the those followers of the Prophets who were first and foremost to believe in them, the martyrs, and the righteous. And how excellent these companions are!"
(Surah an-Nisaa:069)

Dhul-Qi'ddah 9th

Notes

Yunus Ibn 'Abdal-'Alaa said, "Shaafa'ee said to me, 'Oh Yunus, full withdrawal from the people leads to a kind of enmity, yet excessive involvement with them leads to harmful association,-so be one who is between withdrawal and excessive involvement." (Siyaar 'Alaam an-Nubala: vol. 10, page 89)

Notes

"We sent no Messenger, but to be obeyed by Allaah's Leave. If the hypocrites, when they had been unjust to themselves, had come to you -Muhammad - and begged Allaah's forgiveness, and the Messenger had begged forgiveness for them, indeed, they would have found Allaah All-Forgiving- One Who forgives and accepts repentance, Most Merciful. But no, by your Lord, they can have no Faith, until they make you -Oh Muhammad- judge in all disputes between them, and find in themselves no resistance against your decisions, and accept them with full submission." (Surah an-Nisaa:64-65)

Notes

Abu Burda said, "I saw Ibn 'Umar, who was present at the time a Yemenee man was going around the House of Allaah carrying his mother on his back, saying, 'I am for her an obedient camel . If her regular mount was to become scared, I myself would not become frightened. ' Then he came and asked, 'Oh Ibn 'Umar! Do you see that I have repaid her?' He replied, 'No, not even for a single one of her groans during your birth.' Then Ibn 'Umar made tawaf around the House of Allaah, came to the Maqam and then prayed two rak'ahs. He said, 'Oh Ibn Abu Musa, every two rak'ahs makes up for every sin that proceeded from you before performing them.'
(Authenticated by Sheikh Al-Albaanee in Saheeh 'Adab al-Mufrad: 9)

Notes

Yunus As-Sadafee said, "I have not seen anyone more intelligent than Shaafa'ee. I argued with him one day about a specific issue, and then we went different ways. Later he met me and took my hand, and said, 'Oh Abu Musaa! It is only proper that we remain as brothers even though we cannot agree about this issue.'" Imaam ad-Dahahabee said, "The indicates the breadth of the intellect possessed by this leading scholar and his understanding, as the people will never cease disputing and differing with eachother."
(Siyaar 'Alaam an-Nubala: vol. 10, page 16)

Notes

"And whoever contradicts and opposes the Messenger after the right path has been shown clearly to him, and follows other than the believers' way. We shall keep him in the path he has chosen, and burn him in Hell - what an evil destination." (Surah An-Nisa 4:115)

Notes

'Irbaadh Ibn Saariyah said that Messenger of Allaah, may Allaah's praise and salutations be upon him, said, "Whoever of you lives after me shall see much difference of opinion; so adhere to my Sunnah and the Sunnah of the rightly-guided Khaleefahs after me; bite on to it with your molar teeth; and beware of innovations, for every innovation is misguidance." (Authenticated by Sheikh al-Albaanee in Sunan Abu Dawod and Sunan at-Tirmidhee)

Notes

Abu Hurairah reported that the Prophet, may Allaah's praise and salutations be upon him, said, "A child cannot repay his father for his efforts, except if he happened to find him as a slave, purchased him, and then set him free." (Authenticated by Sheikh Al-Albaanee in Saheeh 'Adab al-Mufrad: 8)

Notes

Ahmad Ibn Harb said, "I have worshipped Allaah for fifty years, and I did not discover the sweetness of worship until I turned away from three things: I turned away from the pleasure of the people such that I was able to speak the truth, I turned away from companionship with the wrongdoers such that I found righteous companions, and I turned away from the sweetness of the world such that I would reach the sweetness of the Hereafter."
(Siyaar 'Alaam an-Nubala: vol. 11, page 34)

Notes

Taysala Ibn Mayyas said, "I used to be with some people who were from the sect of the Khawaarij, during which time I committed transgressions that I could now only see now as being major sins. I mentioned that to Ibn 'Umar. He inquired, 'What were they?' I replied, 'Such action and such action.' He stated, 'These are not in fact major sins. There are nine major sins: associating others in one's worship with Allaah, killing someone, desertion from the army when fighting, falsely accusing a chaste woman, spending wealth that is gained from interest, unlawfully using the property that belongs to an orphan, spreading matters which lead others towards apostasy in the masjid, ridiculing others, and causing your parents to cry through your disobeying them.' Ibn 'Umar then said to me, 'Do you wish to distance yourself from the Fire? Do you want to enter Paradise?' I replied. 'Yes, by Allaah!' He asked, 'Are your parents living?' I replied, 'My mother is still alive.' He said, 'By Allaah, if you speak gently to her and feed her what she needs of food, then you will enter the Garden as long as you stay away from the major sins.'"
(Authenticated by Sheikh Al-Albaanee in Saheeh 'Adab al-Mufrad: 6)

Notes

Ibn Taymiyyah, rahimahuAllaah, said, "There is no criticism for the one who proclaims adherence to the way of the early generations, who attaches himself to it and refers to it. Rather, it is obligatory to accept that from him by the unanimous agreement of the Ummah that the way of the first generations is nothing other than the truth." (Majmua' al-Fataawaa 4:149)

Dhul-Qi'ddah 19th

Notes

"So if they believe in the like of that which you believe, then they are rightly guided; but if they turn away, then they are only in opposition. So Allaah will suffice you against them. And He is the All- Hearer, the All-Knower."
(Surah Al-Baqarah:137)

Notes

The Prophet, may Allaah's praise and salutations be upon him, said, "Indeed the Jews split into seventy-one sects, and the Christians split into seventy-two sects, and this Ummah will split into seventy-three, all of them in the Hellfire except for one." They said: "Who are they, Oh Messenger of Allaah?" He said, "Those who are upon that which I and my Companions are upon today."

(Authenticated by Sheikh Al-Albaanee in Sunan Abu Dawud, Sunan Ibn Maajah, and others)

Notes

"There is no good in most of their secret talks except in him who enjoins charity in Allaah's Cause, or the doing of good, or conciliation between people; and he who does this, seeking the good Pleasure of Allaah, We shall give him a great reward."   (Surah an-Nisaa:114)

Notes

Dhul-Qi'dah 23rd

'Umar Ibn al-Khataab said, "Your supplications are halted between the heavens and earth, without anything of them raising further until you add to them the sending of salaams upon your Prophet." (Authentically narrated by Imaam at-Tirmidhee Silsilaat al-Hadeeth as-Saheehah: 2035)

Notes

'Abdullah Ibn 'Umar said, "The pleasure of the Lord lies in the pleasure of the parent. The anger of the Lord lies in the anger of the parent."
(Authenticated by Sheikh Al-Albaanee in Saheeh 'Adab al-Mufrad: 2)

Notes

"Allaah cursed him. And he, Shaytaan said, 'I will take an appointed portion of your slaves. Verily, I will mislead them, and surely, I will arouse in them false desires; and certainly, I will order them to slit the ears of cattle, and indeed I will order them to change the nature created by Allaah.' And whoever takes Shaytaan as a protector or helper instead of Allaah, has surely suffered a manifest loss. He, Shaytaan, makes promises to them, and arouses in them false desires; and Shaytaan's promises are nothing but deceptions. The dwelling of such people is Hell, and they will find no way of escape from it. (Surah an-Nisaa:118-121)

Notes

Dhul-Qi'ddah
26th

"But those who believed, and worked righteousness – We burden not any person beyond his ability – such are the dwellers of Paradise. They will abide therein forever. (Surah al-A'raaf:042)

Notes

Abu Hurairah narrated that the Messenger of Allaah, may Allaah's praise and salutations be upon him, said "I swear by the One in whose hand my soul is. You won't enter the paradise until you believe, and won't believe until you love one another. Wouldn't you like me to guide you to a thing that if you did it, it would make you love one another? Spread the greetings of salaam among yourselves." (Saheeh Muslim)

Notes

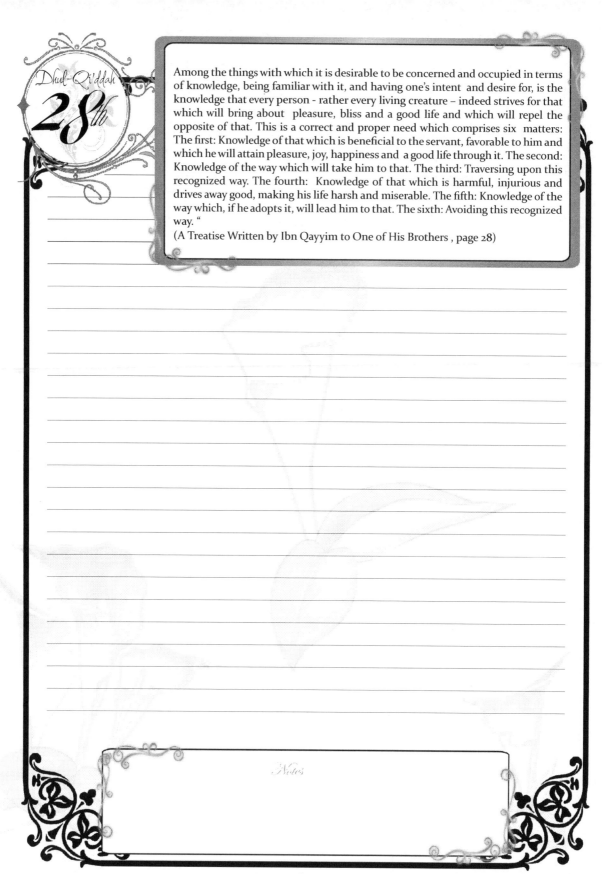

Among the things with which it is desirable to be concerned and occupied in terms of knowledge, being familiar with it, and having one's intent and desire for, is the knowledge that every person - rather every living creature – indeed strives for that which will bring about pleasure, bliss and a good life and which will repel the opposite of that. This is a correct and proper need which comprises six matters: The first: Knowledge of that which is beneficial to the servant, favorable to him and which he will attain pleasure, joy, happiness and a good life through it. The second: Knowledge of the way which will take him to that. The third: Traversing upon this recognized way. The fourth: Knowledge of that which is harmful, injurious and drives away good, making his life harsh and miserable. The fifth: Knowledge of the way which, if he adopts it, will lead him to that. The sixth: Avoiding this recognized way. "

(A Treatise Written by Ibn Qayyim to One of His Brothers , page 28)

Notes

"A worshiper's two feet will not move on the Day of Judgment until he is questioned about four matters: His youth and how he spent it; his knowledge and how he acted upon it; his wealth and how he earned and spent it ,and his body and how he used it."   (Authenticated by Sheikh al-Albaanee in Saheehut-Targheeb wat-Tarheeb (1 126))

Notes

An-Nu'maaan Ibn Basheer narrated that the Messenger of Allaah, may Allaah's praise and salutations be upon him, said, "Supplication is worship." Then he recited the verse, "And your Lord said, 'Call upon me, I will respond to you. Verily those who scorn My worship, they will surely enter Hellfire humiliated.'" (Authenticated by Sheikh al-Albaanee in Sunan Abu Dawud: 1481, Sunan Ibn Maajah: 3828)

Notes

...an extra journal page

Notes

Dhul-Hijjah

1438

AUG / SEP 2017

Yaum al-Sabt Saturday	Yaum al-Ahad Sunday	Yaum al-Ithnayn Monday	Yaum ath-Thulatha Tuesday	Yaum al-Arbo'a Wednesday	Yaum al-Khamees Thursday	Yaum al-Jumi'ah Friday
				1 23	2 24	3 25
4 26	5 27	6 28	7 29	8 30	9 31	10 1
11 2	12 3	13 4	14 5	15 6	16 7	17 8
18 9	19 10	20 11	21 12	22 13	23 14	24 15
25 16	26 17	27 18	28 19	29 20		

You must protect yourself from false notions and if you don't do so then they become ideas, and protect yourself from false ideas because if you fail to do so the will become actual desires. So struggle against them, as if you do not do them they might become your focus and what you resolve to do. As if you fail to fight against this occurring then they eventually become harmful actions which if you do not cure through engaging in their opposite meaning good deeds, they will become your general practice and way, after which it will be very difficult for you to turn away from them.

(Sheikh al-Islaam Ibn Qayyim in his work "al-Fawaid", page 43)

Abu ad-Darda narrated that the Messenger of Allaah, may Allaah's praise and salutations be upon him, said, "Should I not inform you of the best of your deeds, and the purest of them in the view your Master, and the highest of them in the ranks you can reach, and that which is better than your spending gold and silver, and better for you than meeting your enemy and striking their necks, and them in return striking your necks?" They said, "Of course." He said, "The remembrance of Allaah the Most High." Mua'dh Ibn Jabal said, "There is nothing that causes salvation from the punishment of Allaah more than the remembrance of Allaah." (Authenticated by Sheikh al-Albaanee - Sunan at-Tirmidhee: 3377, Sunan Ibn Maajah: 3790)

Notes

Abu Hurairah narrated that the Messenger of Allaah, may Allaah's praise and salutations be upon him, said, "Whoever wishes that Allaah would respond to him during hardship and grief, then let him supplicate often when his state is one of ease."
(Authenticated by Sheikh al-Albaanee- Sunan at- Tirmidhee: 3382)

Notes

Al-Bara' reported that whenever Allaah's Messenger, may Allaah's praise and salutations be upon him, went to bed, he said, "Oh Allaah, it is with Your name that I live and it is with Your name that I die." And when he got up he used to say: "All praise is due to Allaah who gave us life after having taken it from us (meaning sleep) and unto Him is the resurrection."
(Saheeh Muslim: 2083)

Notes

Abu 'Amr ash-Shaybani said, "The owner of this house (and he pointed at the house of 'Abdullah Ibn Masu'd) said, "I asked the Prophet, may Allaah's praise and salutations be upon him, which action Allaah loves best. He replied, 'Prayer at its proper time.' 'Then what?' I asked. He said, 'Then kindness to parents.' I asked, 'Then what?' He replied, 'Then jihad in the way of Allaah.'" He added, "He told me about these things. If I had asked him to tell me more, he would have told me more."
(Authenticated by Sheikh Al-Albaanee in Saheeh 'Adab al-Mufrad: 1)

Notes

"Do not give any consideration to the statements of those who embrace every allowance, those who stop at the least of that which they hold to be an obligation upon them even after others have disputed with them about this- others who consider obligatory that which those who make allowances have abandoned. Perhaps the relevant hadeeths are established and the Prophetic Sunnah is right in front of them, yet they refuse to turn towards that instead saying, 'We are those who only adhere to the saying previous made by so-and-so.' This is something which is not acceptable and correct in the sight of Allaah, and it will not stand as an accepted excuse for the one who opposes what he truly knows from the Sunnah, as Allaah, the Most High, commanded obedience to His Messenger and the following of him alone. He did not command the wholesale following of others besides him. So all others besides the Messenger, may Allaah's praise and salutations be upon him, are only obeyed when they command only that which the Messenger commanded. And everyone besides the Messenger, may Allaah's praise and salutations be upon him, has his statements both accepted and rejected.
(A Treatise Written by Ibn Qayyim to One of his Brothers , page 42)

Notes

Abu Hurairah narrated that the Messenger of Allaah, may Allaah's praise and salutations be upon him said, "...And when he awakens let him say, 'All praise is for Allaah who restored to me my health and returned my soul to me and has allowed me to remember Him.'"
(Authenticated by Sheikh al-Albaanee- Sunan at-Tirmidhee: 3401)

Notes

Narrated By Abu Sa'id al-Khudree : When the Messenger of Allaah, may Allaah's praise and salutations be upon him, put on a new garment he mentioned it by name, turban or shirt, and would then say, "Oh Allaah, for You is all praise, You have clothed me with this, I ask You for the good of it and the good for which it was made, and I seek refuge with You from the evil of it and the evil for which it was made." (Sunan Abu Dawud: 4009, Sunan at-Tirmidhee: 1735-Authenticated by Sheikh al-Albaanee)

Notes

Narrated by Abu Malik Al-Ash'aree : The Prophet, may Allaah's praise and salutations be upon him, said, "When a man goes into his house, he should say: "Oh Allaah! I ask You for good both when entering and when going out; in the name of Allaah we have entered, and in the name of Allaah we have gone out, and in Allaah our Lord do we trust." He should then greet his family. (Authenticated by Sheikh al-Albaanee- Sunan Abu Dawud: 5077 -)

Notes

"...And the fine point of this wisdom was also indicated by Allaah's Messenger of Allaah, may Allaah's praise and salutations be upon him, in the authentic narration concerning the splitting up of this Ummah into seventy-three sects, when he was asked about the saved sect, so he replied, 'It is that which I and my Companions are upon today.' So what is the wisdom in Allaah, the Mighty and Majestic, mentioning the "path of the Believers" in the previous verse, and what is the underlying point of the Messenger of Allaah, may Allaah's praise and salutations be upon him, mentioning his Companions immediately after mentioning himself, in the previous hadeeth? The answer to this is that these noble Companions are the very people who received the two Revelations- meaning the Qur'an and the Sunnah- from the Messenger of Allaah, may Allaah's praise and salutations be upon him, who explained it to them directly- without an intermediary - and this is contrary to all those who came after them...Therefore, it is not possible for any Muslim to independently understand the Book and the Sunnah. Rather one must seek aid in understanding them by returning to the understanding of the noble Companions, who took their understanding from the Prophet, may Allaah's praise and salutations be upon him..." (Sheikh al-Albaanee from al-Asaalah magazine 11,84-87)

Notes

"By Allaah, he does not believe! By Allaah, he does not believe! By Allaah, he does not believe!" It was asked, "Who is that, Oh Messenger of Allaah?" He, may Allaah's praise and salutations be upon him, said, "That person whose neighbor does not feel safe from his evil." (Saheeh al-Bukhaaree: 6016)
'Abdullaah Ibn 'Amr Ibn Al-'Aas narrated that the Prophet, may Allaah's praise and salutations be upon him, said, "Whoever wishes to be delivered from the Fire and to enter the Garden should die with faith in Allaah and the Last Day and should treat the people as he wishes to be treated by them..."
(Saheeh Muslim: 1844)

Notes

"Never would a human being fill a vessel worse than his stomach. It is sufficient for a son of Aadam to eat a few small morsels to support his back. However, if he must eat more, let it be a third of his stomach for food, a third for drink, and a third for breathing." (Authenticated by Sheikh al-Albaanee in Saheehul-Jaami': 5674 and Silsilaat as-Saheehah: 2265)

Notes

'Abdullaah Ibn 'Amr reported that Messenger of Allaah, may Allaah's praise and salutations be upon him, said, "When Allaah deprives one of His believing servants from a loved one- if he displays patience and the seeking of the reward from Allaah, Allaah will not approve for him a reward other than Paradise."
(Authenticated by Sheikh al-Albaanee in Ahkaamul-Janaa'iz: page 34)

Notes

'Ataa Ibn Abee Rabaah reported that Ibn Abbaas asked him, "Shall I show you a woman from the people of Paradise?" He said, "Certainly." Ibn Abbaas then said, "It is this black woman. She came to the Prophet, may Allaah's praise and salutations be upon him, saying, 'I have epileptic seizures, and I get exposed, so ask Allaah to cure me.' He replied, 'If you wish, be patient, and you will be granted Paradise. Or if you wish, I will ask Allaah to cure you.' She replied, 'I will be patient! But I become exposed because of falling, so ask Allaah that I do not become exposed.' So he supplicated to Allaah for her." Ata narrated that he had seen Umm Zufar, that tall black woman, holding the curtain of the Ka'bah.
(Saheeh al-Bukhaaree: 5652, Saheeh Muslim:2576)

Notes

Anas reported that the Messenger of Allaah, may Allaah's praise and salutations be upon him, passed by a woman crying next to a grave. He told her, "Have taqwaa of Allaah, and be patient." Not recognizing him, she responded, "Leave me alone, you have not been struck by an affliction like mine!" She was then told that he was Messenger of Allaah, may Allaah's praise and salutations be upon him. Extremely distressed and agitated at her blunder, she hurried to him and said, "Oh Allaah's Messenger, I did not recognize you." The Messenger of Allaah, may Allaah's praise and salutations be upon him, replied, "Indeed, patience should be displayed at the beginning of the affliction."
(Saheeh al-Bukhaaree, Saheeh Muslim, and others)

Notes

Dhul-Hijjah 15th

"Allaah has promised those among you who believe and do good deeds, that He will certainly grant them ascendancy in the land as He granted it to those before them, and that He will grant them the ability to practice the religion, which He has chosen for them. And He will place in exchange of their fear a sense of security- provided that they worship Me and do not ascribe any partners to Me." (Surah An-Noor: 55)

Notes

Dhul-Hijjah 16th

"And when there came to them a matter concerning public security or fear, they announced it to the people. But if only they had referred it back to the Messenger or to those encharged with authority amongst them, those who have the ability to derive a proper conclusion from it would have understood it." (Surah An-Nisaa: 83)

Notes

And I will never forget what 'Abdul-Qaadir Ash-Shaybaanee, that small ignorant one, said, "We will send some of our brothers to Abee 'Abdur-Rahmaan -meaning Sheikh Muqbil- to get some gulps of knowledge in two months, and then we will send them to some of the centers to take over grounds from the sect of the 'Muslim Brotherhood.'" So I said, "In two months is it possible to produce callers to Allaah??" So if it is such as these ignorant ones that are in charge of directing these groups who claim to call to Allaah, then I give the tidings of the demise of such groups. Rather, we must gather with the scholars and take knowledge from them, as our scholars in the past did. Salmaan Al-Faarisee sat and sought knowledge with the first scholar he encountered until he died, and then a second and a third until he came upon the Prophet, may Allaah's praise and salutations be upon him, and then he followed him. And this is how the companions of Mu'adh were. Before he passed away, they said to him, "Who shall we go to for knowledge after you?" He replied: "To 'Abdullaah Ibn Mas'ood.'" (Sheikh Muqbil Ibn Haadee Al-Waadi'ee in ' Tuhfat-ul-Mujeeb 'alaa As'ilatul-Haadir wal-Ghareeb: page 180)

Notes

"Mu'adh narrated that the Prophet, may Allaah's praise and salutations be upon him, said, "Shall I not tell you how to control all that?" I said, "Yes, do, Oh Messenger of Allaah." So he held his tongue between his fingers, and then he said, "Restrain this." I said, "Oh Prophet of Allaah, are we accountable for what we say?" He, may Allaah's praise and salutations be upon him, said, "May your mother be bereft by your loss! Is there anything more than the harvest of the tongues that throws people on their faces into the Fire?" (Authenticated by Sheikh al-Albanee- Sunan at-Tirmidhee, and others)

Notes

Uqba Ibn Amir said: "I said, 'Messenger of Allaah, what is our best way of surviving?' He, may Allaah's praise and salutations be upon him, replied, 'Guard your tongue, make your house suffice for sheltering your privacy, and weep for your wrong actions.'"
(Authenticated by Sheikh al-Albaanee in Silsilaat al-Hadeeth As-Saheehah: 890)

Notes

Abu Hurairah, may Allaah be pleased with him, related that the Prophet, may Allaah's praise and salutations be upon him, said, "Let whoever believes in Allaah and the Last Day either speak good or remain silent; and let whoever believes in Allaah and the Last Day be generous to his neighbor; and let whoever believes in Allaah and the Last Day be generous to his guest."(Saheeh al-Bukhaaree and Saheeh Muslim)

Notes

Sulayman Ibn Sard said, "I was sitting with the Prophet, may Allaah's praise and salutations be upon him, and two men were slandering one another. One of them was red in the face, and the veins on his neck were standing out. The Prophet, may Allaah's praise and salutations be upon him, said, 'I know a word which, if he were to say it, what he feels would go away. If he said "I seek refuge with Allaah from the Shaytaan," what he feels (i.e., his anger) would go away.'" (Saheeh al-Bukhaaree)

Notes

The Messenger of Allaah, may Allaah's praise and salutations be upon him, said, "If any of you becomes angry, let him keep silent."
(Authenticated by Sheikh al-Albaanee in Saheeh al-Jaame'a: 693, 4027).

Notes

The Messenger of Allaah, may Allaah's praise and salutations be upon him, said, "Whoever controls his anger at the time when he has the means to act upon it, Allaah, then will fill his heart with contentment on the Day of Resurrection." (Authenticated by Sheikh al-Albaanee in Saheeh al-Jaame'a: 6518).

Notes

Dhul-Hijjah
24th

"The best days in the world are the first ten days of Dhul-Hijjah."
(Authenticated by Sheikh al-Albaanee in Saheeh Jaami` us-Sagheer: 1133)

Notes

The Prophet, may Allaah's praise and salutations be upon him, would supplicate, "Oh Allaah, by Your knowledge of the Unseen and Your power over Your creation, keep me alive for as long as You know life is good for me, and cause me to die when You know death is good for me. Oh Allaah, I ask You to make me fear You in secret and in public, and I ask You to make me speak the truth in times of contentment and of anger. I ask You not to let me be extravagant in poverty or in prosperity. I ask You for continuous blessings, and for contentment that does not end. I ask You to let me accept Your decree, and for a good life after death. I ask You for the joy of seeing Your face and for the longing to meet You, without going through diseases and misguiding fitnah (trials). Oh Allaah, adorn us with the adornment of faith and make us among those who are guided. Praise be to Allaah, the Lord of the Worlds."
(Authenticated by Sheikh al-Albaanee in Saheeh al-Jaame'a: 3039)

Notes

"Referring this issue- of the Prophet's birthday celebration- back to the Book of Allaah, we find it ordained upon us to follow the Messenger of Allaah in his Commandments and that He warns us against whatever he prohibits. Furthermore, it tells us that Allaah has perfected the religion for the people. So, as long as this Prophet's birthday celebration is not among the teachings of the Prophet, it cannot be a part of the religion which Allaah has perfected for us and asked us to adhere to by following the Prophet. Again, when we refer this issue back to the Sunnah, of the Messenger of Allaah, we do not find either the Prophet or the Companions doing it by themselves or asking others to do it. So it becomes evident that Prophet's birthday celebration, is not a part of religion, but rather is an innovation and blind imitation of the people of the book- the Jews and the Christians- in their festivals. With this argument in mind, it becomes crystal clear for everyone having the least insight and inclination towards truth and justice, that celebrating any birthday has nothing to do with Islaam. It is rather among the innovations which Allaah and His Messenger warned against emphatically. A wise man must not be deceived by seeing a large number of people doing it throughout the world because the truth is known and recognized by the evidences of Sharee'ah and not by the acts of a great number of people. " (The Milaad:a Caution against Innovation by Sheikh `Abdul `Aziz Ibn 'Abdullaah Ibn Baaz)

Notes

Al-Hasan al-Basree said, "The believer takes care of himself by calling himself to account now for Allaah's sake. As indeed, the easiest accountings on the Day of Judgment are those people who took themselves to account in this world. Whereas the most difficult and oppressive accountings on the Day of Judgment are those people who spent this life without calling themselves to account.... Indeed the believers are a people whom the Qur'an controls and directs such that it intervenes as a barrier between them and that which would cause their destruction. The believer is like a prisoner in this world striving to find that which will ransom him from its bonds. He does not feel secure regarding anything until he knows that Allaah accepts what he has done with his hearing, sight, tongue, and limbs, until He accepts all of this from him."

"Say! Shall we tell you of those who lost most with respect to their actions? Those whose efforts have been wasted in this life, whilst they thought that they were acquiring good by their actions." (Surah al-Kahf:103-104)(As narrated by Imaam Ibn Qayyim in his work 'The Yearned for Relief from the Pursuit by Shaytaan')

Notes

Dhul-Hijjah
28th

"Who is more astray than one who follows his own desires without guidance from Allaah?!"-(Surah al-Qasas:50)

Notes

Shaqeeq al-Balkhee said, "The signs of repentance are that you cry for what you engaged in, have fear of falling into sins, abandon those previous evil companions, and hold fast to good companions."
(Siyaar 'Alaam an-Nubala: vol. 9, page 315)

Dhul-Hijjah
29th

Notes

Dhul-Hijjah
30th

"From the perfection of a person's Islaam is that he leaves alone that which does not concern him."
(Authenticated by Sheikh al-Albaanee in Saheeh at-Tirmidhee: 2318)

Notes

...an extra journal page

Dhul-Hijjah

Notes

MISSION

The Purpose of the 'Nakhlah Educational Series' is to contribute to the present knowledge based efforts which enable Muslim individuals, families, and communities to understand and learn Islaam and then to develop within and truly live Islaam. Our commitment and goal is to contribute beneficial publications and works that:

Firstly, reflect the priority, message and methodology of all the prophets and messengers sent to humanity, meaning that single revealed message which embodies the very purpose of life, and of human creation. As Allaah the Most High has said,

We sent a Messenger to every nation ordering them that they should worship Allaah alone, obey Him and make their worship purely for Him, and that they should avoid everything worshipped besides Allaah. So from them there were those whom Allaah guided to His religion, and there were those who were unbelievers for whom misguidance was ordained. So travel through the land and see the destruction that befell those who denied the Messengers and disbelieved. – (Surah an-Nahl: 36)

Sheikh Rabee'a ibn Haadee al-Madkhalee in his work entitled, '*The Methodology of the Prophets in Calling to Allaah, That is the Way of Wisdom and Intelligence.*' explains the essential, enduring message of all the prophets:

"*So what was the message which these noble, chosen men, may Allaah's praises and salutations of peace be upon them all, brought to their people? Indeed their mission encompassed every matter of good and distanced and restrained every matter of evil. They brought forth to mankind everything needed for their well-being and happiness in this world and the Hereafter. There is nothing good except that they guided the people towards it, and nothing evil except that they warned the people against it. ...*

This was the message found with all of the Messengers; that they should guide to every good and warn against every evil. However where did they start, what did they begin with and what did they concentrate upon? There are a number of essentials, basic principles, and fundamentals which all their calls were founded upon, and which were the starting point for calling the people to Allaah. These fundamental points and principles are: 1. The worship of Allaah alone without any associates 2. The sending of prophets to guide creation 3. The belief in the resurrection and the life of the Hereafter

These three principles are the area of commonality and unity within their calls, and stand as the fundamental principles which they were established upon. These principles are given the greatest importance in the Qur'aan and are fully explained in it. They are also its most important purpose upon which it centers and which it continually mentions. It further quotes intellectual and observable proofs for them in all its chapters as well as within most of its accounts of previous nations and given examples. This is known to those who have full understanding, and are able to consider carefully and comprehend well. All the Books revealed by Allaah have given great importance to these points and all of the various revealed laws of guidance are agreed upon them. And the most important and sublime of these three principles, and the most fundamental of them all is directing one's worship only towards Allaah alone, the Blessed and the Most High."

Today one finds that there are indeed many paths, groups, and organizations apparently presenting themselves as representing Islaam, which struggle to put forth an outwardly pleasing appearance to the general Muslims; but when their methods are placed upon the precise scale of conforming to priorities and methodology of the message of the prophets sent by Allaah, they can only be recognized as deficient paths- not simply in practice but in principle- leading not to success but rather only to inevitable failure. As Sheikh Saaleh al-Fauzaan, may Allaah preserve him, states in his introduction to the same above mentioned work on the methodology of all the prophets,

"So whichever call is not built upon these foundations, and whatever methodology is not from the methodology of the Messengers - then it will be frustrated and fail, and it will be effort and toil without any benefit. The clearest proofs of this are those present day groups and organizations which set out a methodology and program for themselves and their efforts of calling the people to Islaam which is different from the methodology of the Messengers. These groups have neglected the importance of the people having the correct belief and creed - except for a very few of them - and instead call for the correction of side-issues."

There can be no true success in any form for us as individuals, families, or larger communities without making the encompassing worship of Allaah alone, with no partners or associates, the very and only foundation of our lives. It is necessary that each individual knowingly choose to base his life upon that same foundation taught by all the prophets and messengers sent by the Lord of all the worlds, rather than simply delving into the assorted secondary concerns and issues invited to by the various numerous parties, innovated movements, and groups. Indeed Sheikh al-Albaanee, may Allaah have mercy upon him, stated:

"...We unreservedly combat against this way of having various different parties and groups. As this false way- of group or organizational allegiances - conforms to the statement of Allaah the Most High, ◄ *But they have broken their religion among them into sects, each group rejoicing in what is with it as its beliefs. And every party is pleased with whatever they stand with.*►–(Surah al-Mu'minoon: 53) And in truth they are no separate groups and parties in Islaam itself. There is only one true party, as is stated in a verse in the Qur'an, ◄ *Verily, it is the party of Allaah that will be the successful.* ►–(Surah al-Mujadilaah: 58). The party of Allaah are those people who stand with the Messenger of Allaah, may Allaah's praise and salutations be upon him, meaning that an individual proceeds upon the methodology of the Companions of the Messenger. Due to this we call for having sound knowledge of the Book and the Sunnah."

(Knowledge Based Issues & Sharee'ah Rulings: The Rulings of The Guiding Scholar Sheikh Muhammad Naasiruddeen al-Albaanee Made in the City of Medina & In the Emirates – [Emiratee Fatwa no 114. P.30])

Secondly, building upon the above foundation, our commitment is to contributing publications and works which reflect the inherited message and methodology of the acknowledged scholars of the many various branches of Sharee'ah knowledge who stood upon the straight path of preserved guidance in every century and time since the time of our Messenger, may Allaah's praise and salutations be upon him. These people of knowledge, who are the inheritors of the Final Messenger, have always adhered closely to the two revealed sources of guidance: the Book of Allaah and the Sunnah of the Messenger of Allaah- may Allaah's praise and salutations be upon him, upon the united consensus, standing with the body of guided Muslims in every century - preserving and transmitting the true religion generation after generation. Indeed the Messenger of Allaah, may Allaah's praise and salutations be upon him, informed us that, *{ A group of people amongst my Ummah will remain obedient to Allaah's orders. They will not be harmed by those who leave them nor by those who oppose them, until Allaah's command for the Last Day comes upon them while they remain on the right path. }* (Authentically narrated in Saheeh al-Bukhaaree).

We live in an age in which the question frequently asked is, "*How do we make Islaam a reality?*" and perhaps the related and more fundamental question is, "*What is Islaam?*", such that innumerable different voices quickly stand to offer countless different conflicting answers through books, lectures, and every available form of modern media. Yet the only true course of properly understanding this question and its answer- for ourselves and our families -is to return to the criterion given to us by our beloved Messenger, may Allaah's praise and salutations be upon him. Indeed the Messenger of Allaah, may Allaah's praise and salutations be upon him, indicated in an authentic narration, clarifying the matter beyond doubt, that the only "Islaam" which enables one to be truly successful and saved in this world and the next is as he said, *{...that which I am upon and my Companions are upon today.}* (authentically narrated in Jaam'ea at-Tirmidhee) referring to that Islaam which was stands upon unchanging revealed knowledge. While every other changed and altered form of Islaam, whether through some form of extremism or negligence, or through the addition or removal of something, regardless of whether that came from a good intention or an evil one- is not the religion that Allaah informed us about of when He revealed, *❴ This day, those who disbelieved have given up all hope of your religion; so fear them not, but fear Me. This day, I have perfected your religion for you, completed My Favor upon you, and have chosen for you Islaam as your religion.❵*-(Surah al-Maa'edah: 3)

The guiding scholar Sheikh al-Albaanee, may have mercy upon him, said,

"*...And specifically mentioning those among the callers who have taken upon themselves the guiding of the young Muslim generation upon Islaam, working to educate them with its education, and to socialize them with its culture. Yet they themselves have generally not attempted to unify their understanding of those matters about Islaam regarding which the people of Islaam today differ about so severely.*

And the situation is certainly not as is falsely supposed by some individuals from among them who are heedless or negligent - that the differences that exist among them are only in secondary matters without entering into or affecting the fundamental issues or principles of the religion; and the examples to prove that this is not true are numerous and recognized by those who have studied the books of the many differing groups and sects, or by the one who has knowledge of the various differing concepts and beliefs held by the Muslims today."(Mukhtasir al-'Uloo Lil'Alee al-Ghafaar, page 55)

Similarly he, may Allaah have mercy upon him, explained:

"Indeed, Islaam is the only solution, and this statement is something which the various different Islamic groups, organizations, and movements could never disagree about. And this is something which is from the blessings of Allaah upon the Muslims. However there are significant differences between the different Islamic groups, organizations, and movements that are present today regarding that domain which working within will bring about our rectification. What is that area of work to endeavor within, striving to restore a way of life truly reflecting Islaam, renewing that system of living which comes from Islaam, and in order to establish the Islamic government? The groups and movements significantly differ upon this issue or point. Yet we hold that it is required to begin with the matters of tasfeeyah –clarification, and tarbeeyah -education and cultivation, with both of them being undertaken together.

As if we were to start with the issue of governing and politics, then it has been seen that those who occupy themselves with this focus firstly posses beliefs which are clearly corrupted and ruined, and secondly that their personal behavior, from the aspect of conforming to Islaam, is very far from conforming to the actual guidance of the Sharee'ah. While those who first concern themselves with working just to unite the people and gather the masses together under a broad banner of the general term "Islaam", then it is seen that within the minds of those speakers who raise such calls -in reality there is fact no actual clear understanding of what Islaam is. Moreover, the understanding they have of Islaam has no significant impact in starting to change and reform their own lives. Due to this reason you find that many such individuals from here and there, who hold this perspective, are unable to truly realize or reflect Islaam even in areas of their own personal lives in matters which it is in fact easily possible for them to implement. As he holds that no one - regardless of whether it is because of his arrogance or pridefulness - can enter into directing him in an area of his personal life!

Yet at the same time these same individuals are raising their voices saying, "Judgment is only for Allaah!" and "It is required that judgment of affairs be according to what Allaah revealed." And this is indeed a true statement. But the one who does not possess something certainly cannot give or offer it to others. The majority of Muslims today have not established the judgment of Allaah fully upon themselves, yet they still seek from others to establish the judgment of Allaah within their governments...

...And I understand that this issue or subject is not immune from there being those who oppose our methodology of tasfeeyah and tarbeeyah. As there is the one who would say, "But establishing this tasfeeyah and tarbeeyah is a matter which requires many long years!" So, I respond by saying, this is not an important consideration in this matter, what is important is that we carry out what we have been commanded to do within our religion and by our Mighty Lord. What is important is that we begin by properly understanding our religion first and foremost. After this is accomplished then it will not be important whether the road itself is long or short.

And indeed I direct this statement of mine towards those men who are callers to the religion among the Muslims, and towards the scholars and those who direct our affairs. I call for them to stand upon complete knowledge of true Islaam, and to fight against every form of negligence and heedlessness regarding the religion, and against differing and disputes, as Allaah has said, ◌...and do not dispute with one another for fear that you lose courage and your strength departs ◌—(Surah Al-Anfaal: 46).

(Quoted from the work, 'The Life of Sheikh al-Albaanee, His Influence in Present Day Fields of Sharee'ah Knowledge, & the Praise of the Scholars for Him.' volume 1 page 380-385)

The guiding scholar Sheikh Zayd al-Madkhalee, may Allaah protect him, stated in his writing, 'The Well Established Principles of the Way of the First Generations of Muslims: It's Enduring & Excellent Distinct Characteristics' that,

"From among these principles and characteristics is that the methodology of tasfeeyah -or clarification, and tarbeeyah -or education and cultivation- is clearly affirmed and established as a true way coming from the first three generations of Islaam, and is something well known to the people of true merit from among them, as is concluded by considering all the related evidence. What is intended by tasfeeyah, when referring to it generally, is clarifying that which is the truth from that which is falsehood, what is goodness from that which is harmful and corrupt, and when referring to its specific meanings it is distinguishing the noble Sunnah of the Prophet and the people of the Sunnah from those innovated matters brought into the religion and the people who are supporters of such innovations.

As for what is intended by tarbeeyah, it is calling all of the creation to take on the manners and embrace the excellent character invited to by that guidance revealed to them by their Lord through His worshiper and Messenger Muhammad, may Allaah's praise and salutations be upon him; so that they might have good character, manners, and behavior. As without this they cannot have a good life, nor can they put right their present condition or their final destination. And we seek refuge in Allaah from the evil of not being able to achieve that rectification."

Thus the methodology of the people of standing upon the Prophet's Sunnah, and proceeding upon the 'way of the believers' in every century is reflected in a focus and concern with these two essential matters: tasfeeyah or clarification of what is original, revealed message from the Lord of all the worlds, and tarbeeyah or education and raising of ourselves, our families, and our communities, and our lands upon what has been distinguished to be that true message and path.

The Roles of the Scholars & General Muslims In Raising the New Generation

The priority and focus of the 'Nakhlah Educational Series' is reflected within in the following statements of Sheikh al-Albaanee, may Allaah have mercy upon him:

"As for the other obligation, then I intend by this the education of the young generation upon Islaam purified from all of those impurities we have mentioned, giving them a correct Islamic education from their very earliest years, without any influence of a foreign, disbelieving education."
(Silsilat al-Hadeeth ad-Da'eefah, Introduction page 2.)

"...And since the Messenger of Allaah, may Allaah's praise and salutations be upon him, has indicated that the only cure to remove this state of humiliation that we find ourselves entrenched within, is truly returning back to the religion. Then it is clearly obligatory upon us - through the people of knowledge- to correctly and properly understand the religion in a way that conforms to the sources of the Book of Allaah and the Sunnah, and that we educate and raise a new virtuous, righteous generation upon this."
(Clarification and Cultivation and the Need of the Muslims for Them)

It is essential in discussing our perspective upon this obligation of raising the new generation of Muslims, that we highlight and bring attention to a required pillar of these efforts as indicated by Sheikh al-Albaanee, may Allaah have mercy upon him, and others- in the golden words, *"through the people of knowledge"*. Since something we commonly experience today is that many people have various incorrect understandings of the role that the scholars should have in the life of a Muslim, failing to understand the way in which they fulfill their position as the inheritors of the Messenger of Allaah, may Allaah's praise and salutations be upon him, and stand as those who preserve and enable us to practice the guidance of Islaam. Indeed, the noble Imaam Sheikh as-Sa'dee, may Allaah have mercy upon him, in his work, *"A Definitive and Clear Explanation of the Work 'A Triumph for the Saved Sect'"* pages 237-240, has explained this crucial issue with an extraordinary explanation full of remarkable benefits:

"Section: Explaining the Conditions for These Two Source Texts to Suffice You -or the Finding of Sufficiency in these Two Sources of Revelation.

Overall the conditions needed to achieve this and bring it about return to two matters:

Firstly, the presence of the requirements necessary for achieving this; meaning a complete devotion to the Book and the Sunnah, and the putting forth of efforts both in seeking to understand their intended meanings, as well as in striving to be guided by them. What is required secondly is the pushing away of everything which prevents achieving this finding of sufficiency in them.

This is through having a firm determination to distance yourself from everything which contradicts these two source texts in what comes from the historical schools of jurisprudence, assorted various statements, differing principles and their resulting conclusions which the majority of people proceed upon. These matters which contradict the two sources of revelation include many affairs which, when the worshiper of Allaah repels them from himself and stands against them, the realm of his knowledge, understanding, and deeds then expands greatly. Through a devotion to them and a complete dedication towards these two sources of revelation, proceeding upon every path which assists one's understanding them, and receiving enlightenment from the light of the scholars and being guided by the guidance that they possess- you will achieve that complete sufficiency in them. And surely, in the positions they take towards the leading people of knowledge and the scholars, the people are three types of individuals:

The first of them is the one who goes to extremes in his attachment to the scholars. He makes their statements something which are infallible as if their words held the same position as those of the statements of the Messenger of Allaah, may Allaah's praise and salutations be upon him, as well as giving those scholars' statements precedence and predominance over the Book of Allaah and the Sunnah. This is despite the fact that every leading scholar who has been accepted by this Ummah was one who promoted and encouraged the following of the Book and the Sunnah, commanding the people not to follow their own statements nor their school of thought in anything which stood in opposition to the Book of Allaah and the Sunnah.

The second type is the one who generally rejects and invalidates the statements of the scholars and forbids the referring to the statements of the leading scholars of guidance and those people of knowledge who stand as brilliant lamps in the darkness. This type of person neither relies upon the light of discernment with the scholars, nor utilizes their stores of knowledge. Or even if perhaps they do so, they do not direct thanks towards them for this. And this manner and way prohibits them from tremendous good. Furthermore, that which motivates such individuals to proceed in this way is their falsely supposing that the obligation to follow the Messenger of Allaah, may Allaah's praise and salutations be upon him, and the giving of precedence to his statements over the statements of anyone else, requires that they do without any reliance upon the statements of the Companions, or those who followed them in goodness, or those leading scholars of guidance within the Ummah. And this is a glaring and extraordinary mistake.

As indeed the Companions and the people of knowledge are the means and the agency between the Messenger of Allaah, may Allaah's praise and salutations be upon him, and his Ummah- in the transmission and spreading his Sunnah in regard to both its wording and texts as well as its meanings and understanding. Therefore the one who follows them in what they convey in this is guided through their understandings, receives knowledge from the light they possess, benefits from the conclusions they have derived from these sources -of beneficial meanings and explanations, as well as in relation to subtle matters which scarcely occur to the minds of some of the other people of knowledge, or barely comes to be discerned by their minds. Consequently, from the blessing of Allaah upon this Ummah is that He has given them these guiding scholars who cultivate and educate them upon two clear types of excellent cultivation.

The first category is education from the direction of ones knowledge and understanding. They educate the Ummah upon the more essential and fundamental matters before the more complex affairs. They convey the meanings of the Book and the Sunnah to the minds and intellects of the people through efforts of teaching which rectifies, and through composing various beneficial books of knowledge which a worshiper doesn't even have the ability to adequately describe what is encompassed within them of aspects of knowledge and benefits. Works which reflect the presence of a clear white hand in deriving guidance from the Book of Allaah and the Sunnah, and through the arrangement, detailed clarification, division and explanation, through the gathering together of explanations, comparisons, conditions, pillars, and explanations about that which prevents the fulfillment of matters, as well as distinguishing between differing meanings and categorizing various knowledge based benefits.

The second category is education from the direction of ones conduct and actions. They cultivate the peoples characters encouraging them towards every praiseworthy aspect of good character, through explaining its ruling and high status, and what benefits comes to be realized from it, clarifying the reasons and paths which enable one to attain it, as well as those affairs which prevent, delay or hinder someone becoming one distinguished and characterized by it. Because they, in reality, are those who bring nourishment to the hearts and the souls; they are the doctors who treat the diseases of the heart and its defects. As such they educate the people through their statements, actions as well as their general guided way. Therefore the scholars have a tremendous right over this Ummah. The portion of love and esteem, respect and honor, and thanks due to them because their merits and their various good efforts stand above every other right after establishing the right of Allaah, and the right of His Messenger, may Allaah's praise and salutations be upon him.

Because of this, the third group of individuals in respect to the scholars are those who have been guided to understand their true role and position, and establish their rights, thanking them for their virtues and merits, benefiting by taking from the knowledge they have, while acknowledging their rank and status. They understand that the scholars are not infallible and that their statements must stand in conformance to the statements of the Messenger of Allaah, may Allaah's praise and salutations be upon him. And that each one from among them has that which is from guidance, knowledge, and correctness in his statements taken and benefited from, while turning away from whatever in mistaken within it.

Yet such a scholar is not to be belittled for his mistake, as he stands as one who strove to reach the truth; therefore his mistake will be forgiven, and he should be thanked for his efforts. One clarifies what was stated by of any one of these leaders from among men, when it is recognizes that it has some weakness or conflict to an evidence of the Sharee'ah, by explaining its weakness and the level of that weakness, without speaking evilly of the intention of those people of knowledge and religion, nor defaming them due to that error. Rather we say, as it is obligatory to say, "And those who came after them say: ◈ *Our Lord! forgive us and our brethren who have preceded us in faith, and put not in our hearts any hatred against those who have believed. Our Lord! You are indeed full of kindness, Most Merciful.* ◈ -(Surah al-Hashr: 10).

Accordingly, individuals of this third type are those who fulfill two different matters. They join together on one hand between giving precedence to the Book and the Sunnah over everything else, and, on the other hand, between comprehending the level and position of the scholars and the leading people of knowledge and guidance, and establishing this even if it is only done in regard to some of their rights upon us. So we ask Allaah to bless us to be from this type, and to make us from among the people of this third type, and to make us from those who love Him and love those who love Him, and those who love every action which brings us closer to everything He loves."

Upon this clarity regarding the proper understanding of our balanced position towards our guided Muslim scholars, consider the following words about the realm of work of the general people of faith, which explains our area of efforts and struggle as Muslim parents, found in the following statement by Sheikh Saaleh Fauzaan al-Fauzaan, may Allaah preserve him.

"*Question: Some people mistakenly believe that calling to Allaah is a matter not to be undertaken by anyone else other than the scholars without exception, and that it is not something required for other than the scholars according to that which they have knowledge of -to undertake any efforts of calling the people to Allaah. So what is your esteemed guidance regarding this?*" The Sheikh responded by saying:

"*This is not a misconception, but is in fact a reality. The call to Allaah cannot be established except through those who are scholars. And I state this. Yet, certainly there are clear issues which every person understands. As such, every individual should enjoin the good and forbid wrongdoing according to the level of his understanding. Such that he instructs and orders the members of his household to perform the ritual daily prayers and other matters that are clear and well known.*

Undertaking this is something mandatory and required even upon the common people, such that they must command their children to perform their prayers in the masjid. The Messenger of Allaah, may Allaah praise and salutations be upon him, said, { Command you children to pray at seven, and beat them due to its negligence at ten.} (Authentic narration found in Sunan Abu Dawood). And the Messenger of Allaah, may Allaah praise and salutations be upon him, said, { Each one of you is a guardian or a shepherd, and each of you is responsible for those under his guardianship....} (Authentic narration found in Saheeh al-Bukhaaree). So this is called guardianship, and this is also called enjoining the good and forbidding wrongdoing. The Messenger of Allaah, may Allaah praise and salutations be upon him, said, { The one from among you who sees a wrong should change it with his hand, and if he is unable to do so, then with his tongue, and if he is not able to do this, then with his heart. } (Authentic narration found in Saheeh Muslim).

So in relation to the common person, that which it is required from him to endeavor upon is that he commands the members of his household-as well as others -with the proper performance of the ritual prayers, the obligatory charity, with generally striving to obey Allaah, and to stay away from sins and transgressions, and that he purify and cleanse his home from disobedience, and that he educate and cultivate his children upon the obedience of Allaah's commands. This is what is required from him, even if he is a general person. As these types of matters are from that which is understood by every single person. This is something which is clear and apparent.

But as for the matters of putting forth rulings and judgments regarding matters in the religion, or entering into clarifying issues of what is permissible and what is forbidden, or explaining what is considered associating others in the worship due to Allaah and what is properly worshiping Him alone without any partner- then indeed these are matters which cannot be established except by the scholars"

(Beneficial Responses to Questions About Modern Methodologies, Question 15, page 22)

Similarly the guiding scholar Sheikh 'Abdul-'Azeez Ibn Baaz, may Allaah have mercy upon him, also emphasized this same overall responsibility:

"*...It is also upon a Muslim that he struggles diligently in that which will place his worldly affairs in a good state, just as he must also strive in the correcting of his religious affairs and the affairs of his own family. As the people of his household have a significant right over him that he strive diligently in rectifying their affair and guiding them towards goodness, due to the statement of Allaah, the Most Exalted, ◊ Oh you who believe! Save yourselves and your families Hellfire whose fuel is men and stones ◊ -(Surah at-Tahreem: 6)*

So it is upon you to strive to correct the affairs of the members of your family. This includes your wife, your children- both male and female- and such as your own brothers. This concerns all of the people in your family, meaning you should strive to teach them the religion, guiding and directing them, and warning them from those matters Allaah has prohibited for us. Because you are the one who is responsible for them as shown in the statement of the Prophet, may Allaah's praise and salutations be upon him, **{ Every one of you is a guardian, and responsible for what is in his custody. The ruler is a guardian of his subjects and responsible for them; a husband is a guardian of his family and is responsible for it; a lady is a guardian of her husband's house and is responsible for it, and a servant is a guardian of his master's property and is responsible for it....}** Then the Messenger of Allaah, may Allaah's praise and salutations be upon him, continued to say, **{...so all of you are guardians and are responsible for those under your authority.}** (Authentically narrated in Saheeh al-Bukhaaree & Muslim)

It is upon us to strive diligently in correcting the affairs of the members of our families, from the aspect of purifying their sincerity of intention for Allaah's sake alone in all of their deeds, and ensuring that they truthfully believe in and follow the Messenger of Allaah, may Allaah's praise and salutations be upon him, their fulfilling the prayer and the other obligations which Allaah the Most Exalted has commanded for us, as well as from the direction of distancing them from everything which Allaah has prohibited.

It is upon every single man and women to give advice to their families about the fulfillment of what is obligatory upon them. Certainly, it is upon the woman as well as upon the man to perform this. In this way our homes become corrected and rectified in regard to the most important and essential matters. Allaah said to His Prophet, may Allaah's praise and salutations be upon him, ◈ **And enjoin the ritual prayers on your family...** ◈ (Surah Taha: 132) Similarly, Allaah the Most Exalted said to His prophet Ismaa'aeel, ◈ **And mention in the Book, Ismaa'aeel. Verily, he was true to what he promised, and he was a Messenger, and a Prophet. And he used to enjoin on his family and his people the ritual prayers and the obligatory charity, and his Lord was pleased with him.** ◈ -(Surah Maryam: 54-55)

As such, it is only proper that we model ourselves after the prophets and the best of people, and be concerned with the state of the members of our households. Do not be neglectful of them, oh worshipper of Allaah! Regardless of whether it is concerning your wife, your mother, father, grandfather, grandmother, your brothers, or your children; it is upon you to strive diligently in correcting their state and condition..."

(Collection of Various Rulings and Statements- Sheikh 'Abdul-'Azeez Ibn 'Abdullah Ibn Baaz, Vol. 6, page 47)

We hope to contribute works which enable every striving Muslim who acknowledges the proper position of the scholars, to fulfill the recognized duty and obligation which lays upon each one of us to bring the light of Islaam into our own lives as individuals as well as into our homes and among our families. Towards this goal we are committed to developing educational publications and comprehensive educational curriculums -through cooperation with and based upon the works of the scholars of Islaam and the students of knowledge. Works which, with the assistance of Allaah, the Most High, we can utilize to educate and instruct ourselves, our families and our communities upon Islaam in both principle and practice. The publications and works of the Nakhlah Educational Series are divided into the following categories:

Basic / Elementary: Ages 4-11
Secondary: Ages 11-14
High School: Ages 14- Young Adult
General: Young Adult –Adult
Supplementary: All Ages

Publications and works within these stated levels will, with the permission of Allaah, encompass different beneficial areas and subjects, and will be offered in every permissible form of media and medium. As certainly, as the guiding scholar Sheikh Saaleh Fauzaan al-Fauzaan, may Allaah preserve him, has stated,

"Beneficial knowledge is itself divided into two categories. Firstly is that knowledge which is tremendous in its benefit, as it benefits in this world and continues to benefit in the Hereafter. This is religious Sharee'ah knowledge. And secondly, that which is limited and restricted to matters related to the life of this world, such as learning the processes of manufacturing various goods. This is a category of knowledge related specifically to worldly affairs.

…As for the learning of worldly knowledge, such as knowledge of manufacturing, then it is legislated upon us collectively to learn whatever the Muslims have a need for. Yet If they do not have a need for this knowledge, then learning it is a neutral matter upon the condition that it does not compete with or displace any areas of Sharee'ah knowledge…"

("Explanations of the Mistakes of Some Writers", Pages 10-12)

So we strive always to remind ourselves and our brothers of this crucial point also indicated by Sheikh Sadeeq Ibn Hasan al-Qanoojee, may Allaah have mercy upon him, in: 'Abjad al-'Uloom', (page 89)

"…What is intended by knowledge in the mentioned hadeeth is knowledge of the religion and the distinctive Sharee'ah, knowledge of the Noble Book and the Pure Sunnah, of which there is no third along with them. But what is not meant in this narration are those invented areas of knowledge, whether they emerged in previous ages or today's world, which the people in these present times have devoted themselves to. They have specifically dedicated themselves to them in a manner which prevents them from looking towards those areas of knowledge related to faith, and in a way which has preoccupied them from occupying themselves from what is actually wanted or desired by Allaah, the Most High, and His Messenger, who is the leader of men and Jinn. Such that the knowledge in

the Qur'an has become something abandoned and the sciences of hadeeth have become obscure. While these new areas of knowledge related to manufacturing and production continually emerge from the nations of disbelief and apostasy, and they are called, "sciences", "arts", and "ideal development". And this sad state increases every day, indeed from Allaah we came and to Him shall we return....

...Additionally, although the various areas of beneficial knowledge all share some level of value, they all have differing importance and ranks. Among them is that which is to be considered according to its subject, such as medicine, and its subject is the human body. Or such as the sciences of 'tafseer' and its subject is the explanation of the words of Allaah, the Most Exalted and Most High, and the value of these two areas is not in any way unrecognized.

And from among the various areas there are those areas which are considered according to their objective, such as knowledge of upright character, and its goal is understanding the beneficial merits that an individual can come to possess. And from among them there are those areas which are considered according to the people's need for them, such as 'fiqh' which the need for it is urgent and essential. And from among them there are those areas which are considered according to their apparent strength, such as knowledge of physical sports and exercise, as it is something openly demonstrated.

And from the areas of knowledge are those areas which rise in their position of importance through their combining all these different matters within them, or the majority of them. Such as revealed religious knowledge, as its subject is indeed esteemed, its objective one of true merit, and its need is undeniably felt. Likewise one area of knowledge may be considered of superior rank than another in consideration of the results that it brings forth, or the strength of its outward manifestation, or due to the essentialness of its objective. Similarly the result that an area produces is certainly of higher estimation and significance in appraisal than the outward or apparent significance of some other areas of knowledge.

For that reason the highest ranking and most valuable area of knowledge is that of knowledge of Allaah the Most Perfect and the Most High, of His angels, and messengers, and all the particulars of these beliefs, as its result is that of eternal and continuing happiness."

We ask Allaah, the most High to bless us with success in contributing to the many efforts of our Muslim brothers and sisters committed to raising themselves as individuals and the next generation of our children upon that Islaam which Allaah has perfected and chosen for us, and which He has enabled the guided Muslims to proceed upon in each and every century. We ask him to forgive us, and forgive the Muslim men and the Muslim women, and to guide all the believers to everything He loves and is pleased with. The success is from Allaah, The Most High The Most Exalted, alone and all praise is due to Him.

Abu Sukhailah Khalil Ibn-Abelahyi
Taalib al-Ilm Educational Resources

Taalib al-Ilm Educational Publications is looking for

Distributors & Publication Contributors

Distributors:

We are working to make Taalib al-Ilm Education Resources publications available through distributors worldwide. As of 1433 h./2012 c.e. we offer local shipping from North America (United States), Europe & Africa (UK), & South East Asia (Australia), for soft cover, hardcover, as well as ebooks online. We offer quantity discounts worldwide including North and South America, Europe and U.K., Africa, and Asia, on all quantity printed purchases by individuals, masjids, Islamic centers, local study groups, Muslim homeschooling groups, conference vendors, and retail stores according to the following discount scale:

50% discount for order of   **USD**   **$2000** or over

60% discount for order of   **USD**   **$5000** or over

For further information, please contact the sales department by e-mail: *service@taalib.com.*

Publication Contributors:

Additionally, in an effort to further expand our publication library, we are seeking contributing authors, translators, and compilers with beneficial works of any area of Sharee'ah knowledge for submission of their works for potential publication by us. For details and all submission guidelines please email us at: *service@taalib.com*

Referral bonus: *Individuals who refer a new distributor or publication contributor to us can receive a **$25 PayPal payment**, upon a confirmed contract with a publication contributor or receipt of a newly referred distributor's initial order at the 40% discount level. Contact us for further information and conditions.*

Statements of the Guiding Scholars of Our Age Regarding Books & their Advice to the Beginner Seeker of Knowledge

with Selections from the Following Scholars:

Sheikh 'Abdul-'Azeez ibn 'Abdullah ibn Baaz -Sheikh Muhammad ibn Saaleh al-'Utheimein - Sheikh Muhammad Naasiruddeen al-Albaanee - Sheikh Muqbil ibn Haadee al-Waada'ee - Sheikh 'Abdur-Rahman ibn Naaser as-Sa'adee - Sheikh Muhammad 'Amaan al-Jaamee - Sheikh Muhammad al-Ameen as-Shanqeetee - Sheikh Ahmad ibn Yahya an-Najmee

(May Allaah have mercy upon them.) &

Sheikh Saaleh al-Fauzaan ibn 'Abdullah al-Fauzaan - Sheikh Saaleh ibn 'Abdul-'Azeez Aal-Sheikh - Sheikh Muhammad ibn 'Abdul-Wahhab al-Wasaabee -Permanent Committee to Scholastic Research & Issuing Of Islamic Rulings

(May Allaah preserve them.)

With an introduction by: Sheikh Muhammad Ibn 'Abdullah al-Imaam
Collected and Translated by Abu Sukhailah Khalil Ibn-Abelahyi al-Amreekee

[Available: **Now** ¦ pages: 350+ ¦ price: (S) **$25** (H) **$32** ¦ eBook **$9.99**]

Summarized Table of Contents (A Selection of Some Questions)

Guidance and Direction for Every Male and Female Muslim

*The revival of Islaam that we are witnessing: is it simply a reaction to the present corruption and far from Allaah's true way as some have portrayed it? Or is it founded and based upon that which will produce true results, if Allaah wills?   * What is the correct and sound position to be adopted by the scholar, the student of knowledge, and the caller to Allaah in relation to the modern day groups, parties, and "Islamic" organizations?   * Examine, may Allaah have mercy upon you, everything you hear from the people of your age. * Proceed with Caution, Oh caller to the 'Renewal' of the Religion! * Four questions regarding the terms 'Islamic thought' and 'freedom of thought' * Regarding Knowledge: Its Merits, and which Knowledge is Considered Obligatory   * The Prophet Sought Refuge From Knowledge Which Does Not Benefit & Knowledge is of Two Types * The Categories of Knowledge and the Rulings Regarding them & The Ruling of Learning these Various Branches   * Esteemed Sheikh please inform us about the concept of deriving rulings directly from the evidences, and the concept of blind following. What is meant by blind following and what is meant by a scholar independently deriving rulings? Was blind following present in the age of the Companions? and the next generation of the Successors to the Companions? Did some of them blindly follow others from among them in Sharee'ah rulings or not?' * What is the description of those scholars whom we should be guided by? * The Reasons for the Weakness of the Muslims in the Face of their Enemies & the Means to Cure This*

Golden Advice that Benefits the Beginner Regarding Acquiring Knowledge

Should we begin with seeking knowledge or with calling to Allaah? * I want to seek Sharee'ah knowledge and begin studying; however, I don't know how to begin. What do you advise me in this regard? * For the beginning student of knowledge, for example in America, what is your advice regarding those books that he should begin with and then those to proceed to step-by-step? * With what do you advise the one who wants to seek Sharee'ah knowledge but he lives far away from the scholars, knowing, however, that he has a collection of books containing both complete books as well as summarized books? * With what do you advise the one who begins seeking knowledge when he is older in age? Additionally, if it is not easy for him to take knowledge from and sit often with a scholar, will he benefit from seeking knowledge without a scholar? * I have been seeking knowledge for some time; however I do not see its results upon myself or upon my family except to a small degree. So what is the reason for this, and what is the remedy for this situation? * What is best for the students of knowledge: to devote themselves completely to seeking knowledge, and then afterwards fully dedicate themselves to spreading knowledge among the people, inviting their neighbors and those around them to Allaah? Or is it better to seek knowledge for perhaps a month and then to stop studying, due to the need to engage in calling to Allaah and so proceed according to the limits of the knowledge one has acquired? * What are those matters within the methodology of the People of the Sunnah and the Jama'ah which it is permissible to differ in, while giving advice to each other remains; and which matters is it is not permissible for us to differ in? Is it permissible to differ in regards to the basic correct belief, or with the different issues of belief? In what source work can we find a simple clarification of this? * What is the proper way for the student of knowledge to act in situations where there is a difference of opinion in knowledge based issues, in order that unity is maintained between our hearts and conflicts are avoided? * What characteristics should be found within the one whom you wish to take knowledge from? * Are audio cassettes considered a method from the methods of acquiring knowledge? And what ways, for example, can we benefit from them? * The Ideological War: Its Characteristics, Methods & the Required Response to It * What is the Islamic ruling on reading daily newspapers and publications, or magazines, for the purpose of getting societal, Islamic, governmental, or cultural news in order to understand what is going on around us? * Is it permissible for someone to leave working in order to devote himself to seeking knowledge, while the responsibility of his family is upon his father and his brother? * If a student of knowledge receives discouragement regarding his efforts from his family, his wife, and some of his close relatives, what will assist him in shielding himself from this? * Is it permissible for the proficient student of knowledge to declare someone a person of innovation or to declare that someone has in reality abandoned Islaam, or is this a matter exclusively for the scholars? * Is it for the beginning student of knowledge to put forth criticism or praise regarding individuals, or to declare people to be innovators in the religion without relying upon evidence? * Oh Abu 'Abdur-Rahman, we need for you to inform us how you organize your time in seeking knowledge. When do you do your research, when do you teach your brothers, and how many lessons do you have during a day and a night? And we ask Allaah for sincerity of intention for you and for ourselves. * A Basic Summary of the Behavior and Manners of Scholars and Students * If Allaah grants someone success in their efforts of seeking beneficial knowledge and then they return to their land, how should they begin calling to Allaah?

Beneficial Guidance for Female Students of Sharee'ah Knowledge

*What is the Sharee'ah knowledge that it is obligatory upon a woman to learn? * What do you say regarding women and calling to Allaah? * What is the Islamic ruling for a woman who fulfills all the conditions of seeking knowledge within her home, but despite this, she goes to the masjid to meet her sisters in faith or to convey to them knowledge that she has? * If a woman seeks knowledge in the masjid, when she returns home she needs to review what she has learned at the masjid and this takes considerable time. But she knows that work in her home waits for her as she assists her mother in the home. The affairs of her home take all of her time and seeking knowledge needs full dedication from her. So if she is occupied in her home, she is not able to acquire a great deal of knowledge. How can she reconcile between her commitment to her home and her dedication to seeking knowledge? * A woman studies within her home and she prefers to remain in her home- not even going out to the masjid. Is she better, or the woman who seeks knowledge outside and visits different masjids? * What is the ideal example of calling to Allaah by women?*

Guidance from the Scholars Regarding Important Books to Acquire for Seeking Knowledge

*Is it permissible to learn the religion solely from books without the scholars, specifically in the situation when it is difficult to learn from the hands of the scholars because of their scarcity? In addition, what is your view regarding the one who says, 'The one whose teacher is his book his errors are greater than that which he is correct in?' * We see that some people do not give importance to seeking knowledge from the hands of the scholars and are satisfied with studying books in their homes. They argue that Sheikh al-Albaanee (may Allaah the exalted preserve him) was able to reach the level of knowledge that he possesses solely by means of reading, not by means of taking from the scholars themselves. Is this correct and with what do you advise the one who says this? * We live in Britain and are from Ahlus-Sunnah wa al-Jama'ah. However, we do not have any scholars among us; also we only have a few translated books and these are not in the areas of fiqh or the explanation of the Qur'aan. So how should we study, using an acceptable methodology of study, upon the way of the people of the Sunnah and the Jama'ah? What do you advise us in regard to this? * We find that some of the common people and some of the students of knowledge make statements regarding Sharee'ah issues, while not being from the people possessing knowledge of these matters. Then these misguided statements spread among the general people and circulate among them. We need from you, our esteemed scholar, a clarification regarding this issue, so by Allaah what is your view of this? * It is commonly said among some of the people that the one who does not have a scholar, Shaytaan is his scholar. So what is your guidance for them, Esteemed Sheikh? * Which books do you advise us to read in the subject of correct beliefs, the explanation of the Qur'aan, hadeeth narrations and their related sciences, and in the subject of fiqh? * What are considered the most authentic books after the Noble Qur'aan? * Books of Guidance and Books of Misguidance. * What are those books a student of knowledge should begin with, and then those to proceed on to? * Oh Sheikh, we hope that you would name for us some of the books in conformance with the methodology of the first three generations of Islaam that it is proper for the youth upon that clear way to acquire and for him to place within his home library? * We require a good method for reading books. Is it enough to read them a single time or is it necessary to reread books? And if this is indeed necessary, how is this possible considering the large number of books? * Guidelines for Gathering and Maintaining a Beneficial Library * What are the most authentic books through which we know the transmitted accounts from the lives of the Successors of the Companions? * What is the ruling of the Sharee'ah regarding explanations of the Qur'aan known as scientific explanations? And what is the proper Sharee'ah guided relationship between verses of the Qur'aan and matters of scientific research, as there is much controversy regarding this issue? * Notes Regarding the Best Books taken from the Statements of Sheikh Muqbil * Beneficial Notes Regarding Books*

The Warning of the Scholars from the Books of those who have Deviated & the Means and Ways of Going Astray

*What are the guidelines regarding reading the books of the innovators in the religion or listening to their tapes, if they contain benefit? Is it permissible for the common person to listen to the tapes of the preachers from among the innovators, or the people of division and group partisanship, or others similar to them? * As for those who previously were considered to be upon the correct methodology and then deviated from it, is it permissible for us to listen to their tapes or to read their books that they had written in the past, and similarly their recorded lectures? * We observe that some of those who associate themselves with the methodology of the first three generations occupy themselves with criticisms and warning from the astray groups and sects and neglect seeking knowledge, whereas others among them give priority to seeking knowledge and leave the matter of warnings and criticisms. This is such that it has reached the state where those of the second group say, 'Certainly, criticizing is not from the methodology of the people of the Sunnah at all.' So what is correct in this issue? * What is the difference between a statement of criticism and giving advice? * What are the reference books of the people of the Sunnah which are turned to in order to refute the people of innovation in the religion regarding those matters in which they have differed with the people of the Sunnah? * From where do we obtain beneficial knowledge?*

Clear Statements from the Scholars' Advice Regarding Memorizing Knowledge

*What is the correct way of seeking knowledge? Is it to memorize the texts of the different Sharee'ah sciences, or simply to understand them without memorization? We hope for your guidance regarding this, may Allaah the Exalted preserve you. * Which is better for the student of knowledge: to begin with the study of the explanations of the Noble Qur'aan, or the memorization of hadeeth texts or studying the correct understanding and fundamental principles of these two * I am a young man who is almost thirty years old, and I have not completely memorized the Book of Allaah. But I have not ceased being consistent in my memorization, and I ask Allaah for success. Is it better in my efforts to seek knowledge, to memorize the book of Allaah completely, and after completing that to then seek general Sharee'ah knowledge, or to combine between seeking knowledge and memorizing the Qur'aan? * Please guide me to the way that will assist me in memorizing the Book of Allaah. * What is the ruling about the one who recites Qur'aan but makes mistakes in the pronunciation of short vowels? Will he be rewarded for such a recitation? * What is the correct way to memorize the Qur'aan and the ahadeeth? * Which books explaining the meaning of the Qur'aan do you recommend that we read? Also, regarding memorization of the Qur'aan, if a person memorizes and then forgets is there any harm in that? So how can a person memorize and preserve what he has memorized? * What are the causes that assist the student of knowledge in memorization, may Allaah bless you with good? * Preserving Knowledge by Means of Writing it Down * Reviewing what you have Learned Preserves Knowledge*

Issues Related to the Verifiers of Books in our Age

Can we take from the book verifications of Shu'ayb al-Arnout and his brother? Along with the many people who verify the books from our righteous predecessors in this age; there are some verifiers who initially brought forth books in which are found beneficial points regarding general knowledge and correct belief. Then after they became well known among the ranks of youth, they began to bring forth strange statements and inconsistencies. How can the youth deal with this situation where there is little or no warning from the scholars regarding these shortcomings? From these verifiers, as an example, is the Sheikh 'Abdul-Qadir al-Arnaa'out and his verification of "Aqaawel at-Thiqaat" of Karemee. We benefit from his introduction in relation to issues of correct belief and his refutation the distortion of the source texts by Asha'ree sect. However in contrast to this, in his comments within "Saheeh Ibn Hibbaan", he brings forth similar distortions as them of some attributes of Allaah and legitimizes it. So we hope for a warning from these errors, and that you clarify for us the condition and level of some of the authors and verifiers in our time.

Fasting from Alif to Yaa:

A Day by Day Guide to Making the Most of Ramadhaan

By Umm Mujaahid, Khadijah Bint Lacina al-Amreekiyyah as-Salafiyyah With Abu Hamzah, Hudhaifah Ibn Khalil and Umm Usaamah, Sukhailah Bint Khalil

[Available: **1433** -pages: 250+ ¦ price: (S) **$22.5** (H) **$32** ¦ eBook **$9.99**]

Description:

-Contains additional points of benefit to teach one how to live Islaam as a way of life
-Plus, stories of the Prophets and Messengers including activities for the whole family to enjoy and benefit from for each day of Ramadhaan. Some of the Prophets and Messengers covered include Aadam, Ibraaheem, Lut, Yusuf, Sulaymaan, Shu'ayb, Moosa, Zakariyyah, Muhammad, and more! -Recipes for foods enjoyed by Muslims around the world

Some of the subjects discussed include:

The Letter أ : الإحتساب *(al-Ihtisaab) (consciously seeking the reward of Allaah with good deeds)*

The Letter ت : التراويح *(at-Taraaweeh) (the night prayer specific to Ramadhaan)*

The Letter ج : الجود *(al-jood) (generosity)*

The Letter ح : حفظ الجوارح *(hifdh al-jawaarih) (safeguarding the limbs)*

The Letter خ : الخروج من المنزل *(al-khurooj min al-manzil) (leaving the house)*

The Letter ذ : الذكر *(adh-dhikr) (remembrance of Allaah)*

The Letter ش : الشكر *(ash-shukr) (gratitude)*

The Letter ص : صيام الصغير *(siyaam as-sagheer) (the fast of the young person)*

The Letter ط : الطهر *(at-tahr) (purification)*

The Letter ظ : الظمأ الحقيقي *(adh-dhama' al-haqeeqee) (the true thirst on the Day of Judgment)*

The Letter غ : الغفلة *(al-ghaflah) (heedlessness)*

The Letter ق : قراءة القران *(qura'at al-Qur'aan) (reading and reciting the Qur'aan)*

The Letter ك : كظم الغيظ *(kadhm al-ghaydh) (controlling the anger)*

The Letter م : المفطرات *(al-maftooraat) (that which breaks the fast)*

The Letter ه : الهمة العالية *(al-hamat al-'aaliyah) (the high aspirations)*

The Letter ي : يمن الحسنة *(yumn al-hasana)
(the blessings of good deeds)*

....And so on for all the days of this blessed month.

*& A Few Words Concerning the Eid
from Sheikh Saalih Fauzaan*

SCAN WITH SMARTPHONE

PRINT

FOR MORE INFORMATION

SCAN WITH SMARTPHONE

EBOOK

FOR MORE INFORMATION

Fundamentals of Arabic Class for Women Only

An Online Class for Muslim Women Taught by a Muslim Woman

Developed and Taught by Umm Mujaahid Khadijah Bint Lacina al-Amreekiyyah

[Available: **Now** ¦ Schedule: **Open Continual Enrollment**]

Course Features:

* Four Levels of Study & Supplementary Courses

* Limited class size

* Class meets online three times a week with the teacher

* Class moves at a moderate pace to ensure understanding of the concepts presented

* Begins with a short review of the Arabic alphabet, stressing correct pronunciation

* Grammar, morphology, and writing fundamentals

* Focus on understanding what is read and spoken

* Encompasses both speech and understanding

* Numerous exercises, both in class and out, to increase understanding and ability

* Practice in taking notes from Arabic lectures and simple translation

* Additional Out of class assignments and group projects

* Comprehensive reviews

* Periodic quizzes and tests

* End of class test will determine if one can advance to the next class

* Textbooks, dictionaries, and supplementary materials provided as ebooks

* Use of hadeeth texts and other Islamic material for reading,

understanding and translation exercises

* Class forum to make asking questions and doing group assignments easier

* The teacher will be available through email

to answer course questions and assist the students regularly

For more information about availability please visit

arabicforwomen.taalib.com

*Please visit **study.taalib.com** for information concerning other free and fee-based courses.*

A Lighthouse of Knowledge From A Guardian of the Sunnah:
Sheikh Rabee'a Ibn Haadee 'Umair al-Madkhalee [Books 1 & 2]

Collected and Translated by Abu Sukhailah Khalil Ibn-Abelahyi al-Amreekee

[Available: **Now**¦ pages: **380+** ¦ price: (S) **$20** (H) **$27** eBook **$9.99**]]

Book 1: Unity, Advice, Brotherhood & the Call to Allaah

Section 1.

Statements Of Some Of The Guiding Scholars Of Our Age Regarding Sheikh Rabee'a: • [1] Statements of the Leading Scholar, His Eminence, the Guiding Scholar, Sheikh 'Abdul-'Azeez Ibn Baaz, may Allaah have mercy upon him • [2] Statements of the Guiding Scholar, the Reviver and Scholar Of Hadeeth Sciences, Sheikh Muhammad Naasiruddeen Al-Albaanee, may Allaah have mercy upon him • [3] Statements of the Guiding Scholar, The Scholar Of Fiqh, Sheikh Muhammad Ibn Saaleh al-'Utheimeen, may Allaah have mercy upon him • [4] Statements of the Guiding Scholar, The Esteemed Sheikh, And Scholar Of The Hadeeth Sciences, Sheikh Muqbil Ibn Haadee Al-Waada'ee, may Allaah have mercy upon him • A Question Regarding Who are the Scholars that Remain After Those Who Have Died

Section 2.

Regarding Infallibility & Errors • Accepting Advice and Submission to the Truth • An Affirmation that the Scholars of Medina Do Not Consent or Accept the Mistake Made By Any Scholar • Statement Regarding Infallibility and Errors in a Telephone Conversation with Salafees in Indonesia

Section 3.

An Encouragement Toward Good Relations And Harmony & A Warning Against Separating And Differing-Lecture Questions & Answers

Section 4.

The Advice of Sheikh Rabee'a Ibn Haadee Al-Madkhalee to the Salafees Of France • The Response Of Muhammad 'Abdul-Haadee • Advice to My Salafee Brothers in Egypt & Elsewhere • Advice of Sheikh Rabee'a Ibn Haadee Al-Madkhalee to the Salafees Of Algeria • A Telephone Conversation with Salafees in Algeria

Section 5.

Islamic Brotherly Advice to the Salafees in Yemen [1422] • Declaration from the Scholars of the People of the Sunnah and the Jama'ah in Yemen- (Ma'bar, Yemen- 4\12\1428) • Declaration from the Scholars of the People of the Sunnah and the Jama'ah in Yemen - (Hudaydah, Yemen- 1\5\1429) • A Clear Statement of Advice to the Brothers in Yemen [1429] • Additional Statement from Sheikh Rabee'a- Added Ramadhaan 1429 • A New Way of Differing Taken from the Muslim Brotherhood Organization & The Widening of the Area of Disagreement • What is Required in Light of the Guidance of the Sharee'ah When A Tribulation Occurs • Advices Regarding Methodology Which are of the Upmost Importance • Guidance for the Prevention and Cure of Differences

Section 6.

The Call Of Islaam To Brotherhood Between The Believers • General Guidance For The Youth • My Advice to those Responsible for Internet Sites • Heartfelt Advice To the Sons of the Islamic Ummah & the Carriers of the Salafee Call.

Book 2: The Connection with the People of Knowledge, Affairs of Brotherhood & Other Benefits

Section 1.

Praise Of The Scholars For Sheikh Rabee'a From: The Esteemed Sheikh Ahmad Ibn Yahya An-Najmee • The Esteemed Sheikh Muhammad Ibn 'Abdullah As-Subayyal • The Esteemed Sheikh Saaleh Ibn Muhammad Al-Luhaydaan • The Esteemed Sheikh Saaleh Ibn Fauzaan Al-Fauzaan • The Esteemed Sheikh Hasan Ibn 'Abdul-Wahab Al-Banna • The Esteemed Sheikh Ubayd al-Jaabaree • The Esteemed Sheikh Muhammad As-Sowmalee • The Esteemed Sheikh Zayd Ibn Muhammad Al-Madkhalee • The Esteemed Sheikh Muhammad Ibn 'Abdul-Wahab al-Banna • The Esteemed Sheikh Falaah Ibn Ismaa'eel al-Mundikaar

Section 2.

A Selected Listing of The Scholars of Sheikh Rabee'a Who Have Given Him General Permission To Transmit Knowledge • A Selected Listing of The Scholars Known for the Defense of the Sunnah & Exposure of Innovation Whom Sheikh Rabee'a has a Connection to Through His Teachers • A Selected Listing of His Chains of Narration for the Noble Qur'aan •...(and many other similar sections)

Section 3.

Why (Do You Take Such A Position) Towards Sheikh Rabee'a? • A Visit Of Sheikh Rabee'a With The Council Of Major Scholars In The City Of Ta'if • An Account Entitled "What I Have Witnessed In The Lessons Of The Guiding Scholar Sheikh Rabee'a Al-Madkhalee" • The Praise Of Sheikh Rabee'a For The Scholars Of The Sunnah In General • His Praise For Both The Esteemed Guiding Scholars Sheikh 'Abdul-'Azeez Ibn Baaz And The Esteemed Guiding Scholar Sheikh Al-Albaanee Specifically

Section 4.

A Lecture Entitled: "Adherence To The Methodology Of The First Generations" • Additional Comments Upon the Lecture From Sheikh 'Abdul-'Azeez Ibn 'Abdullah Ibn Baaz

Section 5.

The Balance & Moderation of Islaam • A Discussion of the Current Circumstances in Lebanon, Iraaq, and Palestine • My Position Toward Events in Afghanistan and the Talibaan • Nothing Will Liberate Palestine Except that Which Liberated it The First Time • The Poor Present Condition of The Muslims & The Path To Its Rectification

Section 6.

Some Callers Are Not Known To Clearly Adhere To The Way Of The Salaf And So Have Been Warned Or Cautioned Against, Yet Some People Continue To Sit With Them • How One Deals And Works With Those Salafee Youth Who Are Lax In Their Dealings With The People Of Innovation And Describe Those Who Talk About Them As Those Who are Harsh • Guidance Regarding Asking The People For Wealth For The Sake Of The Efforts Of The Calling to Allaah • Do We In Our Time, Deal with the One Who Innovates in the Religion the Same Way as They Did With the Innovators in the First Generations? • Some Of The Students Of Knowledge In Our Time Have A Blameworthy Bias & Attachment To Individuals • The Meaning Of Biased Partisanship (Hizbeeyah) & The Meaning Of The Statement, 'So And So Is Affected By Partisanship' • Regarding The One Who Lies And He Is Not From Those Striving To Rectify Matters • Clarification Of A Statement Of Sheikh Al-Islaam Ibn Taymeeyah • Question Regarding The Excuse Of Ignorance

Section 7.

Why Have You Chosen This Methodology of Criticism and Commendation in Religion As A Path, Despite That Fact That Many Consider It a Cause For Bringing Forth Disunity • The Issue of Warning Is not Restricted Only to the People of Innovation in the Religion • We Warn You Against Injustice, From Engaging In Fabrication, And From Transgressing Against The Honor Of The Ones Whom You Have A Legitimate Dispute With • The Difference Between The Way Of Following The First Righteous Generations And The Path Of Hadaadeeyah • A Summary Of The Issues Of The Hadaadees • Sheikh Rabee'a Exonerates his Son (from among the students) Mu'adh as-Shummaree from the False Accusation of Being From Among the Hadaadees

Section 8.

Regarding The Mistake Of The Scholar • Educating, Cultivating Advice For The Salafees • Mistakes Of Some Of The Salafee Youth

Appendix 1-8 - Selections from the Statements of some of the well known major scholars of this ages

SCAN WITH SMARTPHONE

PRINT

FOR MORE INFORMATION

SCAN WITH SMARTPHONE

EBOOK

FOR MORE INFORMATION

My Hijaab, My Path

A Comprehensive Knowledge Based Compilation on Muslim Women's Role & Dress

Collected and Translated by Umm Mujaahid Khadijah Bint Lacina al-Amreekiyyah

[Available: **Now**¦ pages: **190+** ¦ price: (S) **$20** (H) **$32** ¦ eBook **$9.99**

Table of Contents:

SCAN WITH SMARTPHONE

PRINT

FOR MORE INFORMATION

SCAN WITH SMARTPHONE

EBOOK

FOR MORE INFORMATION

My Home, My Path

A Comprehensive Source Book For Today's Muslim Woman Discussing Her Essential Role & Contribution To The Establishment of Islaam – Taken From The Words Of The People Of Knowledge

Collected and Translated by Umm Mujaahid Khadijah Bint Lacina al-Amreekiyyah

[Available: **Now** ¦ pages: **420+** ¦ price: (S) **$25** (H) **$35** eBook **$9.99**]

Table of Contents:

*Publishers Introduction * Compilers Introduction*

The Role of the Woman and her Significant Influence in Life
by Sheikh 'Abdul-'Azeez Bin Baaz (may Allaah have mercy upon him)
The Role of the Woman in Building the Muslim Society
by Sheikh Muhammad ibn Saaleh al-'Utheimeen (may Allaah have mercy upon him)
The Role of the Woman in Educating and Raising the Family by Sheikh Saaleh Fauzaan
Islaam's Ennoblement of Women by Sheikh Saalih Fauzaan (may Allaah Preserve Him)
Warning against the Forbidden Display of Beauty and Uncovering
by Sheikh Muhammad ibn 'Abdul-Wahaab al-Wasaabee (may Allaah Preserve Him)
Rectification of the Households by Sheikh Muhammad al-Imaam (may Allaah Preserve Him)
My Advice to my Muslim Sisters by Sheikh Jamaal al-Haarithee (may Allaah Preserve Him)

Islamic Ruling Section

Rulings Regarding Beliefs • Rulings Regarding the Role of Women in Islaam
Rulings Regarding Education and Employment • Rulings Pertaining to Work
Rulings Regarding the Household • Rulings Regarding Marriage
Rulings Regarding Polygeny • Rulings Regarding the Children
Rulings Regarding Others

Obligations of the Believing Woman

Her Obligations Towards her Lord • Her Obligations Towards her Parents
Her Obligations Towards her Husband • Her Obligations Towards her Children
Her Obligations Towards her Extended Family
Her Obligations Towards her Neighbors and Companions

Appendices

Appendix 1: Female Students of Knowledge (Parts 1-5)
Appendix 2: The Islamic Rulings Regarding
Free Mixing of Men and Women
Appendix 3: The Family & Principles
of Familial Conduct

SCAN WITH SMARTPHONE

PRINT

FOR MORE INFORMATION

SCAN WITH SMARTPHONE

EBOOK

FOR MORE INFORMATION

BOOK PUBLICATION PREVIEW:

Thalaathatul-Usool: The Three Fundamental Principles

A Step by Step Educational Course on Islaam
Based upon Commentaries of 'Thalaathatul-Usool' of Sheikh Muhammad ibn 'Abdul Wahaab
(may Allaah have mercy upon him)

Collected and Arranged by Umm Mujaahid Khadijah Bint Lacina al-Amreekiyyah

Available: **Now**- **Self Study/ Teachers Edition** pages: 420+ ¦ price: (S) **$27.5** (H) **$35** eBook **$9.99**
Directed Study Edition pages: 320+ ¦ price: **$22.5 Exercise Workbook** pages: 120+ ¦ price: **$12.50**

Description:

*A complete course for the Believing men and women who want to learn their religion from the ground up, building a firm foundation upon which to base their actions. This is the **second** in our* **Foundation Series** *on Islamic beliefs and making them a reality in your life, which began with* **"al-Waajibaat: The Obligatory Matters".**
The course utilizes various commentaries of Sheikh Muhammad ibn 'Abdul Wahaab's original text from the following scholars of our age:

Sheikh Muhammad ibn Saalih al-'Utheimeen
Sheikh Saaleh Ibn Sa'd as-Suhaaymee
Sheikh 'Abdul-'Azeez Ibn Baaz
Sheikh Saalih al-Fauzaan
Sheikh 'Abdullah ibn Saalih al-Fauzaan
Sheikh Muhammad 'Amaan al-Jaamee
Sheikh Saalih Aal-Sheikh (and others)

In addition to various statements of scholars of the Sunnah throughout the centuries

Course Features:

'Thalaathatul-Usool' Arabic text and translation
Twenty-five lessons which discuss such vital topics as "Who is your Lord?"- "Who is your Prophet?"- "What is your religion?"- tawheed -shirk -the pillars of Islaam -the pillars of faith -having allegiance to the believers and how to deal with them, as well as the disbelievers -commanding the good and forbidding the evil -emigration to the lands of Islaam -and many many more. -advice and insight on how to make Islaam a reality in your life -how to put into practice all that you learn in this course Review questions and vocabulary after each chapter as well as quizzes and tests A compilation of points of benefit found throughout the book

(Support and discussion group for students at www.taalib.com)

SCAN WITH SMARTPHONE

PRINT

FOR MORE INFORMATION

SCAN WITH SMARTPHONE

EBOOK

FOR MORE INFORMATION

Made in the USA
Middletown, DE
31 December 2016